NĀGĀRJUNA'S PHILOSOPHY OF NO-IDENTITY

NĀGĀRJUNA'S PHILOSOPHY OF NO-IDENTITY

[With Philosophical Translations of the *Madhyamaka-kārikā Śūnyatā-Saptai* and *Vigrahavyāvartanī*]

RAM CHANDRA PANDEYA
and
MANJU

EASTERN BOOK LINKERS
DELHI : : (INDIA)

Publishers :

EASTERN BOOK LINKERS

H. O.: 5825/7, New Chandrawal,
Jawahar Nagar, Delhi-110007
Ph.: 9811232913

Show Room: 4806/24, Bharat Ram Road,
Darya-Ganj, New Delhi-110002
Ph. 45797575, 9718887575
e-mail: eblindology@gmail.com
ebl.info76@gmail.com
Website: www.eblindology.com

Edition: 2023

Rs.: ₹ 550.00

ISBN: 978-81-7854-180-8

NAGARJUNA'S PHILOSOPHY OF NO-IDENTITY

By **RAM CHANDRA PANDEYA & MANJU**

RESPECTFULLY DEDICATED
to the memory of

Acharya Narendra Dev
Professor T.R.V. Murti
Professor R.K. Tripathi
Pandit Jagannath Upadhyaya

PREFACE

This work represents a part of our research done under a Major Research Project on "Philosophical Foundations of Value Orientation in Teaching" sponsored by the University Grants Commission. In course of our investigations as to what ancient Indian Philosophers thought about the sense of value that a teacher brings into his teaching, thereby maintaining a continuity of tradition (*saṃpradāya*) through generations to follow, we found that there was not much material available in the extant literature on the subject. It is very much true that each philosopher inherits certain values and propagates them with his contributions through his oral or written teachings. But it is a different matter to reflect, not so much upon the nature of those values, as upon the philosophical methodology of teaching adopted for inculcating those values in pupils. We find some stray reflections of this kind in the Upanisadic dialogues but there is hardly any work presenting a systematic study of the subject available to us.

We were surprised when we looked for this kind of treatment in the works of great Buddhist philosophers, particularly those of Nāgārjuna. The works of Nāgārjuna have been studied extensively but scholars so far failed to notice the fact that his magnum opus the *Madhyamaka*-s'*āstra* is actually a work devoted to the exposition of the Buddha's teaching method. The first and the last verses of this work testify to the fact that the Great Teacher (*Vadatāṃ vara*) that the Buddha has adopted a method suited to the propagation of the value of No-Identity (our translation for *Niḥsvabhāvatā*).

Nāgārjuna presents an exposition of this method through the analysis of system-formation and the examination of the role that langauage and logic play in it. His insistence on the fact that Indentity (*sva-bhāva*) cannot be revealed in any system, as it is necessarily bound by the limitation of language expressing it, has presented in its turn a logic consisting of purely formal syntactical and semantical relations. Thus the quest for obtaining Identity will have to be directed towards that realm where langauage, - logic - bound systems do not operate For us, 'therefore,' the realm of S'ūnyatā, as clarified by Nāgārjuna, is indicative of the limitation of language -logic on the one hand and it holds out the availability of an altogether new approach to truth and reality of Identity on the other. All this, as we have understood the views of Nāgārjuna concerning the teaching method of the Buddha, is possible in a new form of life admitting no distinctions of the kind we are used to hold.

This is what we have tried in brief to bring out in the first part of this work. The second part consists of a philosophical restatement (not to be confused with literal translation) of the *Kārikās* of the *Madhyamaka-śāstra* We thought it necessary to provide direct basis for our approach to Nāgārjuna's philosophy of No-Identity by bringing out full and complete English rendering of one of the most difficult text for the first time. By way of explanation of crucial points, explanatory notes have been added, mainly based on Candrakīrti's famous commentary. Of course the text of the *Kārikās* is given for ready reference mainly on the lines of Prof. P.L. Vaidya's edition. In the third part we have given a free translation of Nāgārjuna's *S'ūnyatā-saptat*i based on its Tibetan versions and CHR. Lindtner's translation contained in his *Nagarjuniana*. The second text included here is *Vigrahavyāvartanī* and its translation done independently by us. These two texts, in our opinion, provide effective and valuable exposition of major philosophical points discussed in the *Madhyamaka- s'āstra*.

We have derived great help by way of discussions from many scholars. To them we express our gratitude. We are indebted to Ms. Eastern Book Linkers for bringing out this book as well as its Hindi companion in a short time. We have dedicated this work to revered memory of great Buddhist scholars of our time with whom one or the other of the authors has studied in Varanasi.

Ramchandra Pandeya
Manju

Delhi
Makara–Saṃkrānti, 1991

CONTENTS

Part I

Nāgārjuna's Philosophy of No-Identity. An Introduction

Part II

The Madhyamaka-Śāstra

Part III

Supplementary Reading

PART - I

NĀGĀRJUNA'S PHILOSOPHY OF NO-IDENTITY

AN INTRODUCTION

- The Orientation of the Buddha's Teaching
- The Goal of the Budha's Teaching
- A Quest for Indentity
- Language and Reality
- Language and Logic
- Śūnyatā : An Epistemological Consideration
- The Structure of Nāgārjuna's Philosophy
- Form of Life : Value-Orientation

Nāgārjuna's Philosophy of No-Identity

An
INTRODUCTION

In order to understand the nature of the philosophical enterprises revealed in the text of the *Madhyamaka-s'āstra* by Nāgārjuna one has to understand the exact context in which the foremost treatise of the Mādhyamika School is written. Nāgārjuna's philosophy has been subjected to very unkind and uneven treatment by both ancient as well as modern scholars. Even in the Buddhist fold Nāgārjuna did not enjoy as much respect and reverence as many other old *ācāryas* lika Asaṅga, Vasubandhu, Digṅāga etc. did. The reason for this comparatively low esteem in which Nāgārjuna was placed is mainly provided by his terse, brief and referentially pregant statements and also by the kind of logic adopted, which is leaning towards negative conclusions. The same reason mentioned above, coupled with Brahmanical egoism, depicted Nāgārjuna in the Brahmanical fold as a staunch nihilist, a philosopher having no conclusions but displaying sophistry.

It is true that to a reader ancient or modern Nāgārjuna's statements would appear having no philosophical contents in the form of expressly propounded metaphysics and epistemology. In the absence of any clear philosophical conclusion stated by Nāgārjuna modern scholars are tempted to draw their own conclusion, relating Nāgārjuna's philosophy, on the one hand, to Vedānta-like Absolutism and, on the other hand, to stark nihilism and agnosticism. In the modern times Nāgārjuna's philosophy seems to be like a rudderless ship tossed in the midst of huge waves, currents and cross currents of philosophical argumentation. It is all, as has been pointed out above, due to the methodological peculiarity of Nāgārjuna's philosophical enterprise.

One has to acknowledge the fact that the philosophical method of Nāgārjuna is unique in the history of Indian and Asian philosophy in general and Western philosophy, which commands today a universal respect, in particular. In order, therefore, to understand what Nāgārjuna is addressing himself to, without letting our acquired philosophical understanding interfere, we should look into the method adopted by him in his writings. In fact, some of the scholars have tried to look into his method for some kind of dialectics or to look at it as a method of reductio- ad-absurdum resulting in withering away of all the possible philosophical ideas at the end.

To us there appears a definite positive goal which Nāgārjuna attempts to achieve through his novel method, totally misunderstood and at times maligned. A careful study of the *Madhyamaka-s'āstra* reveals the purpose for writing the book under consideration. Just in the introductory verse of salutation to the Buddha Nāgārjuna pays homage to him who has propounded relational origination, which is said to be the termination of all linguistic descriptions and is quintessence.

Similarly, he concludes the book by paying again his respect to the Buddha who taught *Saddharma*, in order to remove all the views. If we relate thus the first and the last sentences of the book we find that Nāgārjuna is trying to say something philosophically significant concerning the teaching imparted by the Buddha. The Buddha, as a great teacher, imparting intricate knowledge of values for men to follow in their life is therefore indicative of the orientation of his teaching. In this orientation two significant points have been mentioned: one relates to the language which terminates at the kind of value the Buddha has propounded and the other spells out that the value the Buddha is leading to is quintessence. Thus we shall try to look at the value orientation of teaching as stated by Nāgārjuna and the philosophical foundation that he provides in course of his extensive discussions, carried on through twentyseven long chapters.

I

THE ORIENTATION OF THE BUDDHA'S TEACHING

There is no doubt regarding the goal towards which the Buddha was guiding his disciples. It is universally acknowledged that he was concerned with the suffering of all kinds, besetting and threatening the very existence not only of human beings but of the enire sentient beings as well. He took for granted that to be is to suffer and life is the root cause of all the calamities that a living creature has so far faced and is likely to face in countless foreseen or unforeseen manners. It is not a question of life in the present existence; its plight has been continuing in a beginningless process and unless some effective measures are taken in an appropriate manner this plight would continue endlessly. In other words existence by nature is such that it invites calamities for which sometimes he is a free agent, or he acts under compulsion or he does it unknowingly. The Buddha through his teachings draws our attention to this necessary fact of life and in accordance with his wisdom, obtained through his own efforts, he exhorts people to follow a course of life which stears clear of all the sufferings that there could be. Thus taking suffering as a basic fact the Buddha conceives a way out, whereby he separates life from suffering which is associated with it only accidently but not necessarily.

When the Buddha sets on the path of making people see all kinds of suffering, the orientation of his teaching becomes obvious. But there is one more factor without reference to which any talk about the orientation of his teaching would remain incomplete. Though he is concerned with the removal of suffering he is at the same time thoroughly motivated by compassion for all the living beings. To undertake the task of teaching is indicative of pure compassion or mahākaruṇā without which the infinite wisdom of the Buddha would never have assumed concrete from of utterance. Here one may also look into the nature of compassion by which the Buddha is compelled to teach. Since he was expressing that wisdom which he obtained under the Bodhi tree through his own efforts, his wisdom was unrestricted in any and every sense and was thoroughly universal. Its expression through teaching is likewise universal, having no restriction, constraint, bias, prejudice, ulterior motive etc. Inspired by this pure kind of compassion for all living beings, past, present and future, he took upon himself the task of addressing his universal wisdom for the perpetual benefit of all.

In this task of universally compassionate teaching the Buddha has obviously to use a language such that it can serve the purpose of teaching. Thus a couple of other considertions necessarily connected with the act of teaching become important. As there is no language universally understood and since there is no one supreme standard language (as *Saṃskṛta* is understood in the Brahmanical way of thinking) the choice of language on the part of the Buddha was dictated by the kind of audience that he had before him. Even among his audience he had also to keep in mind differnt levels of maturity, understanding and spiritual as well as mental achievements of the people comprising his audience. Being a skilful master teacher the Buddha in course of his teachings was aware of all these factors.

Keeping in view the considerations mentioned above Nāgārjuna took upon himself the task of determining various levels of the Buddha's teaching. He does not think that each and every utterance of the Buddha is meant for all and everything that he says expresses his final opinion. According to Nāgārjuna only one class of the Buddha's teaching spells out his final view. The rest of it is only peripheral and at best can be conceived as methodological tools leading to the final goal. The distinction between those utterances which are meant to attract the people to the path of Buddhist life and those utterances which are meant to attract people to the final goal *(neyārtha* and *nītārtha)* is clearly kept in view by Nāgārjuna in his *Madhyamaka-s'āstra*. Thus the orientation of the Buddha's teaching, according to Nāgārjuna's interpretation given in the *Madhyamaka-śāstra*, is to elaborate and to critically justify the adopted values as revealed in his final level of teaching. In course of his discussion, therefore, Nāgārjuna has also to show why a set of the Buddha's teachings does not belong to his idea of the final truth.

II

THE GOAL OF THE BUDDHA'S TEACHINGS

As has been stated above, the Buddha was concerned with the removal of suffering from life. The main question is why suffering comes to life at all? In the final verdict of the Buddha, people suffer exclusively on account of ignorance of what there is. It is said that not knowing the true nature of a thing people cling to its peripheral and very often sensually attractive aspect, taking it in their considered opinion to be the essence of that thing. It is therefore the duty of a wise teacher to tell the essence from the superficial. Under the spell of ignorance this distinction is lost sight of. Nāgārjuna's main task is to find out what could if any be the essence of things in all coditions (*svabhāva*).

In the fifteenth chapter of his book Nāgārjuna clearly states his idea of *svabhāva*. This idea in fact is repeatedly put forth in the entire work. Nāgārjuna considers it necessary to establish if possible the essential nature of things, so that the same could be cited as the thing and our knowledge and language could conform to it. The essence or *svabhāva* means that aspect of a thing which remains the same throughout and which does not depend on anything else. In other words the essence should be free from causation and change, existing eternally in its own right. It is a different matter that such essence is not available at all because of the universally proclaimed view of the Buddha that any and every existing thing is subject to the law of the relational origination (*pratītyasamutpāda*). This being the case there could not be anything which would be free from the operation of causes and relativity. A thing has a borrowed existence, totally dependent on various factors contributing to the emergence of the thing existing. In this sense a thing having no cause cannot come into being and a thing emerging as a result of operation of causes derives its being from operating causes, having nothing of its own to claim.

It is said that the Buddha made no exception to the universal law of relation. What could be the reason for this, excepting that in the philosophical system he was constructing there was no place for eternal entities. One foremost reason that we find in various texts is that eternal entities invite permanent attachment or aversion, which is an important source of suffering. Moreover, since it would not be possible to explain the reason why an eternal thing would come into existence, its eternality would defy our understanding which is necessarily condemned to operate within the sphere of relationality. Human mind according to the Buddhist analysis seeks to understand one thing only in relation to others. An eternal thing existing in its own right would not relate itself to anything else. The essence, if any, has to be necessarity eternal and thus non-relational. But at the same time it would be a great source of suffering by causing attachment. It is this reason that the Buddha and his followers had in mind while rejecting the notion of enernality.

It is also a curious but inevitably necessary event that the passion for permanence and eternality makes people blind to the fact of change. They very often take really changing phenomena to be permanent. Change is the way of life but permanence gives meaning to it. However, change is real and permanence is appearance. Appearance is not to be taken as reality which when very often happens in life is due to ignorance. Thus, the essence of a thing is not at all linked with reality and in no way essence affects the changing nature of reality. Essence or *svabhāva* is thus a view, a *dṛṣṭi* wrongly formed, mistaking a thing for the real.

In this way in the teachings of the Buddha man's quest for essence is shown to be natural to him, because he thinks the essence to be a meaning or value of existence. The teaching of the Buddha seeks to remove this view of essence. The Buddha taught that essence has to be discarded, as it is a disvalue. Rather the orientation of his teaching is towards inculcating the value of essencelessness, to be realized by removing all such view-points which have no connection with reality.

III

A QUEST FOR IDENTITY

Philosophy is a quest for identity. Identity is to be defined as the essence of a thing. In fact the Mādhyamika would not make a distinction between a thing and its essence, because this would imply that there could be a thing without essence also. In fact instead of saying 'the essence of a thing' we should say 'thing-in-essence'; but then also this may imply a thing-not-in-essence. Therefore, the nearest expression acceptable to the Mādhyamika would be 'thing-essence' or 'simple essence', whereby complete identity of a thing is possible. This may be an interpretation of the word '*svabhāva*'.

The aim of the Mādhyamika is to find out this essence or identity. Several attempts have been made to pin-point this identity. Philosophers have constructed various theories and adopted various means, like *pramāṇas*, to find out this identity.

In all these cases language has been used as a tool which serves two purposes:

1. To took for identity in the perspective of a constructed theory which aims at imparting consistency and uniformity to the nature of things whose identity is sought. This implies that theories are capable of manifesting identity in terms of consistency with the elements making a theory and also they insure uniform presentation of a thing, by eliminating accidental adjuncts.

2. Language being a necessary expression of, as well as a condition for, any theory dictates, to a great extent, the formation of a theory. Thus a theory is no less an outcome of the langualge adopted than the thought expressed through it. Infact, since every thought is to be expressed through language, the linguistic mode of expression would necessarily govern the structure of a theory. Therefore, identity if at all is to be found, it will have to be within the framework of theory as expressed through a linguistic structure. Moreover, other philosophers have taken for granted that the theory in language reveals the essence of a thing. Mādhyamikas question both these assumptions.

Nāgārjuna shows in the *Madhamaka-s'āstra* that any theory that we construct in order to find out the identity of a thing fails to penetrate deep into the essence. It is rather an opaque veil which does not allow us to have an intimacy with the essence. A theory is by its nature about a thing and 'being about' it cannot be a substitute for the thing. This is what is designated in the Mādhyamika system as *saṃvṛti*.

In the same way the expression of a theory through language is nothing but an enlargement of the theory-content as well as ramification of the linguistic structure. The word *prapañca* is used in the sense of enlargement which ultimately relates only to what is being expressed i.e. a theory, and not to what is there in essence, paramārtha. Saṃvṛti always is inextricably expressed through the structure of a language and thus language is an enlargement only of the theory, not of the essence. To conclude, therefore, any theory and linguistic description associated with it cannot give as even a glimpse of the essence. Nāgārjuna tries to show that the essence cannot be obtained through a theory and language. The purpose of true philosophy is to show that theory and its expression invariably fail to give us the knowledge of thing-essence or identity. This negative result of philosophy also shows by implication that identity is to be sought in the realm transcending language and theorization.

It is an important question to ask whether any constructed theory reveals identity of the thing or whether it is only about the thing. Nāgārjuna's answer to the first alternative is in the negative, mainly because about one and the same thing there can be different theories. For example, in the first chapter Nāgārjuna considers two main theories concering the phenomena of causation. It fact in the case of causation the relation between two things, A and B, is conceived in the light of pre-conceived notion of causation, which is itself a primordial theory-construction of human mind. Any further construction of a theory in terms of the effect being entirely a new creation or it being only a modification of its cuase is a further theoretical construction. Thus in the case of causation a two-tier construction of theory is involved. In this situation the phenomenon of A followed by B remaining the same, alternative theories are constructed, implying thereby that any theory of this type does not stand for the real structure of the phenomenon. Had this been the case no alternative theories would ever be possible. Moreover, between two or more alternative theories there are basic points of conflict and contradictions. Had a theory been the reflection of a situation no variation of any kind would have been permitted. It means that according to Nāgārjuna there is no necessary connection between a phenomenon and a theory. In the final analysis Nāgārjuna therefore holds that theories are about phenomenon representing the point of view that the promulgators of theories have in their mind. In this way the idea of theory is invariably linked, not with the thing itself but, with a view -point (*dṛṣṭi*). In order to understand the true nature of a thing or phenomenon, isolating it from any intervening viewpoint, one has to totally discard the viewpoint underlying theories. Hence in the opinion of Nāgārjuna the Buddha is praised as a great teacher because he seeks through his teaching the true, direct and final knowledge of a thing.

By implication Nāgārjuna shows that the best teacher is he who leads his disciples direct to the thing or to its identity. In this process he also wanted to show the futility of all the theories coupled with viewpoints in relation to the identity of a thing. It is therefore necessary, in order to grasp the sprit of the Buddha's techings, to know why so called theory about things fails to lead to the truth. Hence criticism of theories becomes necessary for the proper understanding of the truth. It is in this spirit that Nāgārjuna has undertaken the task of rejecting all the theories, as they fail to give us the knowledge of truth. At the same time he shows at every step that a thing viewed in the light of a theory will only display a lack of identity or *niḥasvabhāvatā*.

A theory consists mainly in viewing a thing in relation to other entities or to its own chracteristics, functions, etc. It, therefore, necessarily contributes something of its own to the thing which it is about. To make this point more clear let us take the example of the Vais'eṣika theory of *padārtha*. In actual situation a concrete thing, like a flower, is given to us in a unitary form but when it is looked at from the point of view of a theory it no longer remains one unit; it becomes a highly complex entity consisting of *dravya*, *guṇa*, *karma* and *sāmānya* and their inter- relations of all kinds, including *saṃyoga* and *samavāya*, as well as containing within it the absence of everything that there does not exist or is other than itself. Apart from the extension of its own nature it also consists of many kinds of relations that it has with other totally different entities like *ākās'a, kāla* dik, etc. As an object of knowledge, again, it displays its relation to the sense-organ, *manas* and *ātman* and in this context it also carries the values of various kinds like *sukha, duḥkha, grāhya, agrāhya,* beauty, ugliness etc., connected with *icchā, dveṣa, prayatna, dharma* and *adharma;* culminating into its relation to the past impressions or *saṃskāras.* Thus a simple thing like a flower is viewed in such a complex manner and its name 'flower' is only a short reminder to the complex theory within which it is placed. This being the case the total picture under a theory no longer presents before us a simple entity like a flower; a complexity of things is what a theory compells us to look at. Here we may also note that the complexity created by one theory is not a universally acceptable scheme. It is rather one among many alternative schemes possible. Thus a theory not only imparts many extraneous elements but it also admits improvements, substitutions, alternation, as well as alteration

Nāgārjuna in course of extensive review of various theories presented to him concerning any given phenomenon shows at every step that any element drawn from a theory lacks in content; because the theoretical framework is unable, as if to touch that phenomenon. In other words no theory can make any authentic presentation of truth. Statement of a theory is only a statement of the framework within which a thing is viewed. A view generates an elaborate theoretical framework and statement of this theoretical framework, in its turn, can lead only upto this view, no further. The realm of truth always defies being trapped in that framework and remains what it really is (*tathatā*). This element in the philosophy of Nāgārjuna has been linked with various philosophical viewpoints. The Buddha refused to answer certain questions and preferred to remain silent because these questions demanded a trans-theoretical answer vis-a-vis tathatā. Thus, for example, the question 'Whether the Buddha remains after death' if answered within any given theory will not be authentic; but an attempted authentic answer could be given which would not be subjected to any distortion or variation in terms of adopted theory. Now, the Buddha's silence, which is a part of the Buddha's teaching, is interpreted in terms of the weakness of theoretical approach by Nāgārjuna. This approach, however, has been further linked with other theories, like Absolutism, Nihilism, Agnosticism, and what not. To apply these theoretical frameworks to Nāgārjuna's way of approaching the Buddha's silence is to go against the very basis of Nāgārjunian thinking. This attempt rather confirms the view that delusion (*moha*) created by a theory is hard to overcome.

Implicit in the approach of Nāgārjuna outlined above is another interesting point which relates to the idea of *niḥsvabhāvatā* or the lack of identity, as has been stated that any approach through a theory will really remain without content, and thus will not reveal the identity of the thing. At best it may show how a theory would look at it, rather than what a thing is in its pure essence. This is what is in short, the idea of *niḥsvabhāvatā. Niḥsvabhāvatā* is therefore not a total denial of identity. It is the denial of that identity which is presented through a theory.

IV

LANGUAGE AND REALITY

As is the case with a theory so is the character of language used, which describes a thing in a double framework. On the one hand a language states implicity or explicitly something in accordance with the theoretical framework of its speaker. On the other hand there is a pure linguistic framework as well to which a language conforms. Regarding the first point we may also remember that any theory is made concrete only by language in which it is expressed. In fact there is nothing like a theory worth a name which remains unexpressed. A theory is an offspring of language and language is the guide for a theory to proceed. They are thus necessarily interlinked.

One cannot be separated from the other. Here, the second point becomes relevant. Language has been called *prapañca* and truth is *niṣprapañca*. Any language is thus ramification of some- thing, i.e. a thing or idea or a phenomenon. It, therefore, by its own nature amplifies, like a theory, what there is by importing various considerations in course of its progress. In this connection we may briefly review two points concerning language, viz. the relation of language to a thing and its own logic of procedure.

The prevailing opinion regarding the relation between language and the thing meant by it is that language becomes meaningful only when there is some connection between the two. According to some philosophers, like the followers of Nyāya, this connection is established by the will of some conscious agent, like God. In order to make a word meaningful someone has to start the convention of a word meaning a thing. According to other philosophers, like the Mīmāṃsakas and Grammarians, the connection between the two is eternal in the sense that a word as such can have a status only when it is capable of meaning a thing. In this case meaning is the general capacity that a word bears to refer to anything concrete or abstract. In the former case there is a very strong sense of reference which can, in the primary sense, be satisfied only in the context of concrete things where it is possible to demonstrate that a word means that things to which the initiator of a language can point. Only in a weak sense an abstract thing could also be an object of reference by relating that abstract to a concrete entity. Thus, for example, according to Nyāya, the word 'cow' primarily means a concrete particular entity and the reference to the universal cowness in made only through that particular in which the universal inheres. In the case of the other theory of meaning, however, the general capacity of a word consists in reference to a general, universal entity, where either particularity is not needed or if at all present is meant by the word only in a secondary sense. In both these cases, therefore, language is conceived as a necessarily referential phenomenon, implying that a meaningful language requires the presence of a world containing corresponding entities. Meaningfulness of a word is indicative of the presence of an entity in a possible world.

The connection between a word and a thing meant by it is further strengthened by another considertion. Just as a word refers to a thing, similarly a thing worth the name, also stands in need of a word for itself. Anything that could ever be conceived of, including the absence of a thing, is called a *padārtha* or what is meant by a word. The Naiyāyikas, the Mīmāṃsakas and the Grammarians along with the followers of Sāṃkhya-Yoga cannot accept any entity which by its nature defies its allegiance to language. This is necessary because in these systems language is the most powerful tool for establishing the identity of a thing, both in the contexts of knowledge as well as communications. A thing is what it is, a matter which can be settled only by resorting to the language which would state all kinds of relations, characteristics and other complexities of the form mentioned earlier. Even to know a thing as merely 'this' we require a language without which a thing under reference cannot be identified, i.e., singled out from the rest of things present. Thus being *padārtha* the identity of a thing cannot otherwise be established.

In the case of the Advaita Vedānta also the standard referential view holds good. But there is a point of special consideration concerning the role of language in establishing the identity of things. Accordingly, there are two ways in which identity can be established. So far as things other than Brahman are concerned the role of language as a tool of imparting identity is accepted to be the same as outlined above. But according to the Advaita Vedānta language is not the sole means for establishing identity. In the case of pure consciousness, free from all connections, language cannot operate, as it is effective only when a thing referred to admits of its relation with other things. But in this case where pure consciousness is the same as Brahman, identity is revealed in self-awareness, which is the state having not even the rudimentary subject-object relation. Thus for Brahman there is no language in the referential sense, but its identity is revealed in self-awareness.

Thus the relation between language and reality is referential according to all the non-Buddhist schools, required for the purpose of establishing the edentity of what there is. But at the same time we may also note that there is non-linguistic identity as well as in the case of the Advaita Vedānta. In keeping with his view concerning the role of theories as stated in the last section, Nāgārjuna attacks the referential theory of meaning with vigour. His main objection against the referential theory of meaning is that the linguistic pattern being exclusively determined by its own dynamism cannot have any concern with the reality it is supposed to refer to. According to him linguistic behaviour is autonomous in so far as it proceeds only according to its use. Linguistic use is detemined, on the one hand, with the convention as to what is to be said in a given situation and, on the other hand, its structure is controlled not by anything external to it but by inherent syntactical and semantic relations. We find Nāgārjuna using these two ideas in course of his examination of various ideas and concepts. For example, the concrete situation hardly warrants the use of two words, for one and the same flower, in the expression 'Here is a flower'. Actually in all such cases flower is not given in isolation from its existence in given space and time. But in a concrete linguistic usage we cannot do without separating an entity from its existence, space and time. Knowledge that we get form these linguistic expressions creates an illusion in our mind that a thing is different from its qualities, relations, motion, universal etc. This is how language leads us away from concrete situation in which it is used, resulting in the positing of entities, which are purely linguistic, upon the concrete entity present. Even where no such separation is ever possible language creates one on its own like 'a barren woman's son'. Here the non-existent son cannot have any relation with the barren woman, still language creates an illusion that there is a relation between the two. Thus what language says is never a guarantee for what actually there is. For Nāgārjuna this is a necessary as well as sufficient ground for holding the view that there is no referential connection between language and reality, as language behaves strictly in accordance with its own inherent rules and procedures.

In keeping with the language Nāgārjuna was familiar with, we find that the pattern of linguistic behaviour is based on the subject-predicate division, which is analogous to the ontological division of substance and quality. Accordingly in any given linguistic expression no subject can be talked about in isolation from its predicates, just as no substance can become an object of knowledge without its qualities. Such an artificial division creates further artificial sub- division of purely linguistic nature. Syntactical relations are thus to be understood purely in terms of linguistic categorisation and these syntactical relations are intermixed with semantical formats of language. According to the Mādhyamika approach one can describe the entire field of linguistic operation in terms of semantical and syntactical categories and their interrelations.

The so-called situation of the speaker pointing to a thing and saying 'Let this word mean this thing', is not the way in which language functions. We, for example, can never find a demonstrable entity called causation (*pratyaya*) behaving like a peg on which the statement 'A is the cause of B' could be hanged. In this connection it may also be noted that in course of his philosophical activity Nāgārjuna amply demonstrates that all expressions are strictly non- ontological, as for example, his repeated statement that an existing thing cannot act and a non-existing thing cannot be acted upon. Similar is his oft-repeated statement that an existing thing cannot be caused, a non-existing thing also cannot be caused and there is nothing in-between existing and non-existing thing which could be caused. Such expressions of Nāgārjuna show that the categories generated by the use of our language need not and cannot have any connection with extra-linguistic world of existence

V

LANGUAGE AND LOGIC

Keeping in view the points elucidated above the famous position of the *Prasaṅga*-Logic becomes clearer. Because of the absence of relation between language and reality any linguistic expression is incapable of saying anything authentic about what there is (tathatā). Therefore no non- linguistic proposition (*pratijñā*) can be asserted. No amount of effort can provide any guidance by means of offering proof etc. so far as the nature of thing is concerned; language cannot say anything about anything. Any statement in its true sense is a statement about language itself and its meaning is totally governed by the linguistic context in which it is used. The linguistic context here means the theoretical construction of a particular kind for which a particular type of language is adopted. This is exactly what is meant by *prasaṅga*, in contrast to the position holding that the language functions within extra-linguistic situation (*svatantra*). In the latter case a linguistic statement, *pratijñā*, is free from the context of language because it seeks to go over to the realm of reality which is free from the bondage of language. This is what is called the *svātantrika* position. As Nāgārjuna does not subscribe to the view of language of the *svātantrika* type, it is his bounded duty to show why a proposition or *pratijñā* in any given situation fails to say anything about extra-linguistic world. Thus he invented a scheme of four-fold expression (*catuṣkoṭi*). In this scheme, four general alternatives are arranged in such a way that no room for any other possible expression is left.

These four expressions, viz., 'is', 'is-not', 'both is and is-not', 'neither is, nor is not', are based upon the observation of linguistic behaviour of subject-predicate form. Here one can see that in each one of these schematic expression existence is supposed to be a predicate, whereas to which it is predicated remains outside the predicate. In all these four expressions, therefore, the subject remains the same, whereas it can assume connection with four exclusive expressions, thereby making it impossible to assert more than one at a time. If four different philosophers are found making assertions of these four kinds about the same subject, then it is very easy to place them side by side, thereby showing without any effort that one and the same thing is being described in four differnt ways. Since a thing is what it is, it cannot admit of more than one predication which shall define its identity. Four possible expressions would therefore obviously reject each other, as identity can be only one of them. Moreover, in case one kind of statement is made the possibility of other kinds of statement cannot be ruled out. This being the case each one of the possible statement would be in order and none of them can be accorded any priority treatment. Logic being based on any specific assertion of one of the four kinds would, therefore, fail to prove anythings. There would be as many systems of logic as there are possible ways of expressions. Hence in exclusive context confined only to one kind of assertion a logic may be helpful but because the function of a teacher is to review all the possible positions he cannot adopt one kind of logic for the examination of other kinds of statements. Therefore, acccording to the scheme of *catuṣkoṭi* the behaviour of language is exposed and analysed thread-bare in order to show that language and logic based on it are ineffective tools, so far as the nature of reality is concerned.

There is a difference between asserting a proposion, *pratijñā*'and mentioning it as made by others. In the latter case the person who mentions does not commit himself as to its truth value and is also not required to justify or to defend it. He is at liberty at the same time, however, to analyse and examine it. This is what Nāgārjuna does in contrast to those who have made original propositions. Nāgārjuna states in his *Vigrahavyāvartanī* that he does not make any proposition. Therefore the burden of justifying it does not fall on his shoulders. This statement however raises an interesting point, which is also relevant for understanding his view on *catuṣkoṭi,* as outlined above. The point relates to the tool of analysis and criticism of the propositions made by others. The question is whether the task of any analysis or criticism of propositions made by others could be undertaken without accepting some basic rules of analysis, which have to be necessarily in the form of propositions themselves. For example, to say that affirmation and denial cannot be held together or to say that the law of the excluded middle cannot be violated, amounts to making a proposition cantaining those rules. Nāgārjuna emphatically denies this allegation by implicitly maintaining a distinction between two levels of propositions of rules. At the first level of assertion the rules are *applied* but at the second level rules are *formed* keeping the first level propositions out. Thus the second level propostions are empty of any assertable or deniable contents. If a person simply mentions propositions made by others and at the same time applies the second level rules, he is keeping himself aloof from the question of truth and falsity in both the moves. In fact in the case of those philosophers who make propositions by following the rules, there is a tendency to obliterate the distinction of levels and to treat both the propositions and the rules applied to them as belonging to the same level. As a result these philosophers have to hold that like the propositions made, the rules also have reference to reality. The law of contradiction or that of the excluded middle is thus supposed to derive its truth-value from the wold of reality. This idea has been expressed in his own way by Nāgārjuna in the *Kārikā* twenty-four of the *Vigrahavyāvartanī*. The ultimate position to which Nāgārjuna seems to subscribe is that such rules of logic which are about propositions can be held and applied and at the same time criticism of propositions made by others can be undertaken without making oneself any proposition of the first level. Thus when he says he does not make any propositions he is talking of only the propositions of the first level. This also means that such a logic would be possible which is purely formal, i.e. which does not take into consideration the truth value of any propositions. In this sense Nāgārjuna is the first philosopher to hold the possibility of a purely formal logic, based on syntactical and other formal relations for logical operations.

In the light of Nāgārjuna's approach to logic and language one can say that the Mādhyamika philosophy is devoted to the framing of the postulates of critical philosophy. Its criticism aims always at the statement made by others, which are shown to have no connection whatsoever with reality, though the makers of these statements claim their referential relation. Since referentiality is denied outright and meaning is shown to be a purely formal property based on the use of language, the function of philosophy is conceived to be negative one. Philosophy, it seems, for the Mādhyamika, is a way to show that identity of essence of a thing cannot be achieved through any enterprise where language is the main stay. Quest for identity within the realm of language is futile and any attempt to find it through language is bound to be frustrated.

VI

S'ŪNYATĀ : AN EPISTEMOLOGICAL CONSIDERATION

The rejection of ontology on the basis of language and logic is further strengthened by Nāgārjuna's approach to epistemology. This point is extensively discussed in the *Vigrahavyāvartanī*. He takes the position that the validity of empirical knowledge is relational, as it depends on the relation between the subject and the object. The object of knowledge is authenticated on the basis of the operation of the process of knowledge being completed. A thing in contact with sense-organs and mind generates perceptual knowledge and this perceptual knowledge by virtue of having revealed that thing guarantees the presence of the object of perception. Thus, those who subscribe to pramāṇa as means for establishing a thing have to hold that knowledge is an evidence for the presence of a thing; but they cannot answer the question cogently as to how this knowledge itself be called valid without reference to the thing which it seeks to validate, as it is stated clearly in the kārikā fifty-two of the *Vigrahavyāvartanī*. On account of this kind of difficulty besetting validity of empirical knowledge and also because of language being a necessary factor in every knowledge, Nāgārjuna questions the very notion of knowledge as a valid means for evidence of an object. Thus in keeping with his formalistic approach to language and logic Nāgārjuna rejects the entire idea of validity vis-a-vis empirical knowledge. For him, therefore, validity does not provide identity to knowledge; it only indicates the general trends of human behaviour. This situation is brought by him in conformity with his theory of *niḥsvabhāvatā,* as for him all empirical knowledge is only a working approach to life. It is in this context that human knowledge is conceived as empty of any guarantee for a thing being there. This is what he seems to think when he says that since knowledge cannot guarantee any validity, it is *s'ūnya*. Being incapable of guaranteeing validity implies also that it connot likewise guarantee invalidity. Hence epistemic notions of validity and invalidity, linked with the view of identitilessness, spells out Nāgārjuna's position of *śūnyatā*. Any view-point which human mind forms and epistemological tools adopted to justify it is called empty of validity-content. *S'ūnyatā,* therefore, is the purgation of validity and identity content from human knowledge.

In the light of our discussions so far Nāgārjuna seems to use the notion of relational origination as it reveals itself at the level of theory formation, as *niḥsvabhāvatā*, and at the emistemological level as *s'ūnyatā*. It is therefore clear that *śūnyatā* and *niḥsvabhāvatā* are different only in terms of their respective fields of applications. If viewed in the light of relational origination they are fully interchangable; at the linguistic level the same idea assumes the form of contextual expression (*upādāya prañjapti*).). This is also a way of conceiving human life where every extreme position on the basis of viewpoint already formed is also to be avoided. The sole idea is concisely stated in 24/18 of his *Madhyamaka-sāstra*

Nāgārjuna is thoroughly consistent in his approach and he does not spare even the followers of the Buddha. He goes to the extent of applying his philosophical tool to such specific ideas of Buddhism as bondage, liberation, *nirvāṇa*, twelve links, *skandha*, and so on. In every case he comes out with the demonstration of hollowness of ideas as expressed in language. The total impact that his philosophy leaves on the mind of his readers is that he is propounding a nihilistic philosophy. In his approach to epistemology also he created the impression that reality cannot be known. But, as we have tried to clarify the position of Nāgārjuna in terms of his views on logic and language, we cannot agree to the charge of nihilism and agnosticism against him. He is, in short, not a nihilist because he holds the view that language, the system of ideas and views expressed through language cannot give us identity of things. Similar is the position that our empirical knowledge being as it is relational cannot guarantee absolute validity to it. To say that language cannot lead us to identity can, by no canon of logic, mean that there is no identity at all. It only means that identity can be achieved by some means other than system-formation and language-manipulation. Similarly the relationality of knowledge only means that validity is to be sought through non-relational knowledge, if that be possible. We have, therefore, to look into the philosophical structure of Nāgārjuna in order to see whether any indications are available in respect of positive contents of the same.

VII

THE STRUCTURE OF NĀGĀRJUNA'S PHILOSOPHY

Let us see the way in which Nāgārjuna has sturctured his philosophical position, specially in arranging his chapters in the *Madhyamaka-s'āstra*. There are in all twenty-seven chapters each one of them called *parīkṣā*. *Parīkṣā* is the examination of different ideas, like that of relationality (*pratyaya*) or viewpoint (*dṛṣṭi*). Here examination consists mainly in the analysis and criticism of cencepts and ideas held by different philosophers. In this sense it is looking (*īkṣā*) all around (*pari*). In the arrangement of his chapters apparently there does not seem to be any design or structure involved. All the known commentators of Nāgārjuna have paid no attention to the arrangement of chapters, implying that each chapter is devoted to one or the other concept taken either arbitrarily or for its prominence in a particular system. We veture to suggest, however, that there is some method involved in selecting twenty-seven concepts and arranging them in the order given in the book.

An examination, as Nāgārjuna shows by implication, has to be in terms of relationality (*pratyaya*) and proceed through the analysis of different concepts, ultimately resulting into the exposition of a viewpoint (*dṛṣṭi*). The aim seems to be to suggest that any concept selected is ultimately linked with a viewpoint and any philosophical position is basically an extension of this viewpoint. Relationality is applicable to the viewpoint and to all its extensions in the form of various concepts and ideas. Thus there seems to be a design in the arrangement of chapters in the *Madhyamakās'āstra*. It appears that Nāgārjuna is trying to show that entire theoretical operation of human mind, right from the conception of change (Chapter-II) to the viewpoint which moulds this conception (Chap. XXVII), through various intermediaries like sense-organ, relation, identity, suffering, bondage, *nirvāṇa,* noble truths etc. are without exception predicated to relationality. In this sense the Mādhyamika philosophy of Nāgārjuna aims at unfolding potentiality of relational origination which is the subject matter of the Buddha's teaching.

VIII

FORM OF LIFE : VALUE ORIENTATION

The analysis of the teaching method adopted by the Buddha in terms of *s'ūnyatā*, identitilessness, as well as non-referentiality of language has been praised by Nāgārjuna, a Buddhist himself. The praise is not in vain; not for branding the Buddha as a nihilist or an agnostic. For Nāgārjuna this philosophy leads to the removal of all these points. This leaves the question open 'What for?'. Why is it that the viewpoints are to be removed, as taught by the Buddha? The answer is given in various forms: that the removal of view-point leads to the removal of suffering. There is no substantial change involved here, excepting the change in the way of looking at things. The line of demarcation between the life of suffering and life free from suffering is not drawn by bifurcating two entirely opposite worlds, i.e., the world of mundane life (saṃsāra) and the world of liberation (ṇirvāṇa). Thus the removal of view-point does not result into the obliteration of one life and the creation of another life. As Nāgārjuna says (25. 19) there is no distinguisting mark between the two lives because there is not the slightest difference between the categories of *saṃsāra* and *nirvāṇa*. This means that for Nāgārjuna *saṃsāra* and *nirvāṇa* do not represent two different ontological or epistemological categories. This is again in keeping with the formalistic and anti-metaphysical approach as outlined above.

What is that form of life which distinguishes the life of suffering from the life of tranquillity? In other words what is that magic in the teaching of the Buddha which makes life full of suffering to become the life of quietitude (*s'iva*)? It is, as Nāgārjuna has been emphasising, a very simple device. We have only to learn to look at the extension of human mind as not involving any real connection with things. We have to simply learn that human thinking, language, logic and any operation of life does not involve identity. Thus the teaching of the Buddha is oriented towards the value of identitilessness in this life.

The value of identitilessness of all human operations when realized is all that the Buddha taught. But philosophers have been indulging in the game of looking for identity that may lie beyond identitiless life. In other words they demand an answer to the question as to whether through the realization of identitilessness some identity is achieved. Some, like Prof. T.R.V. Murti, tend to assert that the denial of identity at the level of ordinary life leaves the real undeniable identity of truth open. This is what is called the Absolute. In the light of our discussion so far, calling Nāgārjuna's philosophy of *śūnyatā* as Absolutism is the greatest blunder and Nāgārjuna has called this blunder as incurable (13.8). Similarly those interpreters who take Nāgārjuna's philosophy to be a form of nihilism commit the same blunder, though in a more serious way. They take identitilessness to be the only end of human thinking; but as we have seen *niḥsvabhāvatā* has only a limited field of operation; it operates only within the sphere of language and relational thinking. It cannot say that human life ends with the end of language and relational mind. If it is possible to conceive of non-relational mind *(prajñā)* and a non-linguistic mode of its cultivation and extension (*upāyā*) the possibility of any person becoming the Buddha cannot be ruled out. But this kind of *prajñā* and *upāya* to achieve it cannot be talked about even by the Buddha; he leads people definitely through his teaching to the realization of that value. Nāgārjuna has provided extensively the philosophical foundations for the exposition of the value-orientation of the teaching of the Buddha by pleading for the cultivation of identitiless form of life.

PART II

NĀGĀRJUNA

THE MADHYAMAKA - ŚĀSTRA

Philosophical Re-statement

Explanatory Notes

Text of the Kārikās

Kārikā Index

A PHILOSOPHICAL RESTATEMENT OF NĀGĀRJUNA'S

MADHYAMAKA-ŚĀSTRA

CHAPTER - I

PRATYAYA-PARĪKṢĀ

An Examination of Relativity

1.2 I pay respects to the best among speakers who, having attained enlightenment, has taught relative origination, which is no-cessation, no-origination, no-annihilation, no-abiding, no-one-thing, no-many-thing, no-coming-in, no-going-out; being the termination of linguistic description, it is the Good.

2. There are nowhere such things which are ever originated; neither by themselves, nor by others, nor by both, nor are they without a cause.

4. There are four relativities, viz., cause, support, non-mediation, and predominance; there is no fifth relativity.

5. The identity (*svabhāva*) of things does not exist in relativity etc. In the absence of own identity there is no identity obtainable from others.

6. Action has no relativity; action does not have non-relativity. On the other hand, relativity does not have no-action as well as action.

7. The relativity is so called because depending upon it something originates. But when there is no origination, why is it not no-relativity?

8. Neither an existent nor a non-existent thing could justifiably have relativity. What could be relativity in respect of a non-existent thing, and what could relativity do in respect of an existent thing?

9. When an identifying character (*dharma*), be it existent or non-existent or both existent and non-existent, does not produce, then this being the case, how could a cause justifiably be the producer?

10. This identifying character is proclaimed to be present without support. Now, the identifying character being without support, how could, then, there be a support?

11. When identifying characters do not originate, it is not proper to talk of cessation. Therefore, it is not proper to have non-mediation. What kind of relativity could there be in respect of a thing which has ceased to be.

12. Because there is no existence of things having no identity; 'this being, that exists' - this (formula) cannot be established.

13. The effect does not exist in relativity taken in isolation as well as in conjunction. How could that come from relativity which does not exist in relativity?

14. (If the idea is that) even though non-existent, the result comes about from that relativity, then why does the result not come about from no-relativity?

15. (It may be held that) the result is a transformation of relativity and the relativity is not what itself it is. The result, which comes about from those which are what they themselves are not then how could that (result) be a transformation of relativity?

16. Therefore, the result is neither a transformation of relativity, nor a non-transformation of relativity. In the absence of the result, how could relativity and no-relativity be possible?

CHAPTER - II

GATĀGĀTA-PARĪKṢĀ

An Examination of going and not-going

1. That which is already traversed is not being traversed at present; that which is not yet traversed is not being traversed at present. There is nothing, other than what has been traversed and what is not yet traversed, which is being traversed at present.

2. (It may be said that) where there is movement (*ceṣṭā*), there is traversing. Because that movement exists neither in what is already traversed, nor in that which is not yet traversed, but only in that which is being traversed. Then traversing is possible only in respect of that which is being traversed.

3. How could the traversing of what is being traversed be justified, when it is not possible to justify two traversings in respect of that which is being traversed?

4. To him who holds that traversing is possible in respect of that which is being traversed, there would arise an inconvenient implication (*prasajyate*) that a path is being traversed without there being the act of traversing because only that is being traversed, which is still in the process of being traversed.

5 There would be two traversings in respect of that which is being traversed: One is the object of the act of traversing, (the path being traversed) and, the second is, the act of traversing existing there.

6. There would be two agents of traversing, when there are two acts of traversing. The reason is that the act of traversing cannot be justified by rejecting the agent of traversing.

7. If the act of traversing is not justified, because the agent of traversing is ignored then, in the absence of the act of trversing, how could there be an agent of traversing?

8. One who goes, does not go; he who does not go cannot go. Who the third, other than the one who goes and the one who does not go, does go?

9. How can the statement 'The goer goes' be justified when it is not justified to hold a non-going goer?

10. He who holds the position 'The goer goes', will have to accept that there is a goer without going; if he desires to uphold the going of the goer.

11. If the goer goes then there would be two goings: The one by virtue of which the person is called 'goer' and the other which makes him the goer, while he is going.

12. Traversing does not start in respect of what is already traversed; traversing does not start in respect of what is not yet traversed. It does not start in respect of what is at present being traversed. Where does traversing start?

13. Before the act of traversing starts, there is no traversing, nor is there something already travered such that in respect of which traversing could start. How is traversing possible in respect of that which is not yet traversed?

14. When the beginning of the very act of traversing remains totally unperceived, how is it imagined as to what is that which is already traversed, what is that which is not yet traversed?

15. The goer does not stay; non-goer does not stay; who the third, other than the goer and the non-goer, would stay?

16. How could the statement 'The goer stays' be justified, when it is not possible to have a goer who is not going?

17. A person does not stay away from what is being traversed, nor from what is already traversed and nor from what is yet not traversed. Going, the beginning of it and staying away are like the act of going.

18. It is not proper to say: 'Going is the same as the goer'. It is not proper to say: 'Goer is different from going'.

19. If going be the same as the goer, then the agent and the action would become identical.

20. If it is imagined that the goer is different from going, then there would be going without the goer and a goer without the act of going.

21. When two things are either jointly or severally not established, how could they both be established?

22. The act of going, by virtue of which a goer is so called, does not go that act of going itself, because the goer is not prior to the act of going, as someone goes some place.

23. The person, called a 'goer' by virtue of one act of going, does undertake another act while going; as when one person goes, he cannot justifiably undertake two acts of going.

24-25 An existing goer does not go in three possible modes; a non-existing goer also does not go in three possible modes. The goer who is existing, as well as non-existing, does not go in three possible modes. Therefore, going, goer and what is to be gone to do not exist.

CHAPTER - III

CAKṢURĀDI-INDRIYA-PARĪKṢĀ

An Examination of Sense-Organs

1. There are six sense-organs viz., the organs of seeing, hearing, smelling, tasting and touching, as well as mind. The objects of their cognition are seeable things etc.

2. Seeing cannot see itself. How can that which cannot see itself, see the others?

3. The example of fire is not sufficient to establish seeing. Because the same, along which seeing, is refuted on the line of the refutation of the path being traversed, the path which has already been traversed and the path which has not yet been traversed.

4. If there is no seeing which does not see, how can the statement 'Seeing sees' be justified?

5. Seeing does not see; non-seeing also does not see. One should also know the explanation of the seer on the line of seeing.

6. There is no seer in disregard to seeing; nor there is one without disregard to seeing. How could there be to you an object of seeing, and seeing when there is no one to see?

7. Just as a son is said to be born relative to father and mother, in the same way consciousness is said to be born relative to the eyes and the form (*rūpa*).

8. In the absence of the object of seeing and seeing, consciousness etc., which are four in number, cannot exist. How then could there be any material (*upādāna*) etc.?

9. Hearing, smelling, tasting, touching and mind could also be explained on the same line as seeing. One should also understand in the same way the agent of hearing, the object of hearing, etc.

CHAPTER - IV

SKANDHA-PARĪKṢĀ

An Examination of the Aggregates

1. No form (*rūpa*) is available free from the cause of the form. The cause of the form is also not seen free from the form.

2. If the form were to be free from the causes of the form, then it would make the form devoid of cause; but there is no entity anywhere without a cause.

3. If the cause of the form were to be free from the form, then the cause would be without an effect; but there cannot be any cause without an effect.

4. There being a form, the cause of the form cannot be justified. In respect of the form having no being, the cause of the form cannot be justified.

5. The form without its cause cannot, can never, be justified. Therefore one should not posit any construction (*vikalpa*) in respect of the form.

6. The statement 'The effect is similar to cause' cannot be justified. In the same way, the statement 'The effect is not similar to its cause' also cannot be justified.

7. Feeling, awareness, consciousness and impressions: all these entities in all respects, have positions similar to the form.

8. In debate, after rejecting with the help of *s'ūnyatā* if someone were to suggest the way to avoid it, then this way could not be avoided, because it would be identical with what is to be proved.

9. In expositions, after explaining with the help of *s'ūnyatā,* if someone were to raise an objection, then that would be no objection, because that could be identical with what is to be proved.

CHAPTER - V

DHĀTU-PARĪKṢĀ

An Examination of Elements

1. There is no *ākāśā* prior to the characteristics of *ākāśā*. If it were prior to the characteristics then it could be without characteristics.

2. There is no entity, nowhere, which is without characteristics. If an entity without characteristics be non-existent, then where would the characteristics apply.

3. The characteristics cannot apply to the entity with or without characteristics. It cannot relate to anything other than the entity, with or without characteristics.

4. If the characteristics cannot relate, then there is nothing having those characteristics. If a thing having characteristics is not justified, then the characteristics are not possible.

5. Therefore, there is neither any entity having characteristics, nor the characteristics themselves. Also there is nothing which could be neither a characterised entity nor the characteristics themselves.

6. In the absence of an entity, whose absence would be in order? Who would having the opposite of existence or non- existence as characteristics know existence or non-existence?

7. Therefore, *ākās'a* has no existence, no non-existence, nor is it a characterized entity, nor the characteristics. The other five elements are like *ākās'a.*

8. People of low intelligence, who see existence or non-existence of entities, cannot see the Good, which is the quintessence of all that could be perceived.

CHAPTER - VI

RĀGARAKTA-PARĪKṢĀ

An Examination of Attachment and its bearer

1. If the person attached were to exist before attachment, having no concern with attachment, attachment would be dependent upon the person attached; as there has to be a person attached that attachment would arise.

2. If the person having attachment does not exist, how will attachment exist? As is the case with existence or non-existence of attachment, so is the position with regard to the person attached.

3. It is not justified to say that attachment as well as the person attached come into being simultaneously, because attachment and the person attached would become independent of each other.

4. If the two are identical, they cannot exist together. The same thing cannot exist with itself. If the two are different, how could they be said to exist together?

5. If the two are identical and yet exist together, then it could exist even without its companion. If the two were different and yet were to exist together, then also one could exist without its companion.

6. If the two are differnt but exist together, then, it may be asked, whether separate existence of attachment and the person attached is established; as only in that case they could have existence together.

7. If the existence of attachment and the person attached is established separately, then why do you conceive togetherness of the two ?

8. Because, as separate existence is not established, you want their togetherness. Then in order to establish their togetherness, you would like to prove their separate existence.

9. Togetherness cannot be established, if separateness is not demonstrated. What kind of separateness being there you would like to accept their togetherness?

10. In this way, on the basis of the person attached, you cannot establish attachment on account of togetherness or separateness. Like attachment, all entities also cannot be established as being together or separate.

CHAPTER - VII

SAṂSKṚTA-PARĪKṢĀ

An Examination of Composite Entities

1. If origination is composite (*saṃskṛta*) then it is proper to say that it has to have three characteristics. If origination is non-composite (*a-saṃskṛta*) then how would the characteristics of composites be possible?

2. Origination etc. the three separately, are not capable of characterzing *composites*. If the three together were to characterize it, then how could they exist at one place and at the same time?

3. If the characteristics of *composites* be another origination, stability and destruction, then this would lead to infinite regress. If, on the other hand, they be not different from it, then they cannot be *composites*.

4. (The opponent may say) The origination of origination is simply the origination of the first origination. The first origination then gives rise to the origination of origaination.

5. (The Mādhyamika says) If the origination of origination is, for you, originated by the original origination, then how would you account for that origination, not brought about by the original origination, giving rise to the original origination?

6. If, according to you, it is originated by the original and orginates the original, then how would the original origination having not been originated by it would originate?

7. Be it that the original origination, having itself been originated, creates another origination, provided that which itself is not originated could originate something.

8. (The opponent may say) Just as a lamp illumines itself as well as others, similarly origination would originate both itself and others.

9. (The Mādhyamika says) Darkness does not exist either in the lamp or at the place where it is located. What could the lamp illuminate? Illumination is the destruction of darkness.

10. How could the lamp, which is being originated, destroy darkness, when the lamp being in the process of origination cannot reach darkness?

11. If darkness is removed by the lamp without having reached it, then that lamp, while staying at its own place, would destroy darkness existing in all the worlds.

12. If lamp illumines itself and others, than there would be no doubt that darkness would also cover itself and others.

13. How could this origination, itself not originated, originate itself? If it originates after having been originated, then having already been originated, why would it be originated again?

14. Neither that which is being originated, nor that which has already been originated, and, not that which is not yet originated can, in anyway, originate. This point has been stated as in the case of that which is being traversed, that which has already been traversed and that which is not yet traversed.

15. When that which is being originated cannot be related to origination, how could we say of a thing being originated in relation to origination?

16. Everything that originates relatively is by nature quiet. Therefore that which is being originated and origination itself are quiet.

17. If there be any unoriginated entity anywhere, the same could originate. But itself being non-existent, what will originate?

18. If origination were to originate that which is being originated, then which origination would originate the previous origination?

19. If another origination were to originate it, then it would lead to infinite regress. If it is originated without origination, then everything would be originated.

20. It is not proper, therefore, as has been explained earlier, to say that an existing thing or a non-existing thing or which is both existing and non-existing thing can originate.

21. The origination of an entity itself being destroyed cannot be justified. No such entity can be justified which is not being destroyed.

22. Nothing exists which is existent; nothing exists which is non-existent; nothing exists which is in the process of existing. What unoriginated entity could have existence?

23. The existence of an entity which is being destroyed cannot be justified. It is also not possible to justify an entity which is not being destroyed.

24. When all entities always have the characteristics of decay and destruction, what are those entities which could have existence without decay and destruction?

25. If existence be due to another existence, then that other existence cannot be justified, as origination of origination is not possible by itself or by something else.

26. That which is not destroyed cannot have destruction; that which is already destroyed also cannot have destruction. That which is in the process of destruction is also of the same type. How could that which is not yet produced be destroyed?

27. The destruction of an existing entity cannot be justified. Similarly the destruction of a non-existing entity also cannot be justified.

28. That very condition which makes the existence possible cannot destroy itself. Another condition which makes the existence of one entity possible cannot destroy the condition of another entity.

29. When in this way the origination of all the entities cannot be justified, the destruction of all the entities, also, likewise, cannot be justified.

30. It is not justified to say that an existing entity is destroyed. When the entity is one, existence and non-existnece in respect of the same cannot be justified.

31. Also the destruction of a non-existent entity cannot be justified, as the second head cannot be cut off.

32. There is no destruction by a thing itself; nor there is destruction brought about by another thing; just as the origination of origination is neither by itself nor by virtue of something else.

33. Because origination, existence and destruction cannot be established, there is no composite entity. When there is no composite entity established how could a non-composite entity be established?

34. Origination, existence and destruction are exemplified in the fashion of magic, dream and a city appearing in the sky (*gandharvanagara*).

CHAPTER - VIII

KARMAKĀRAKA-PARĪKṢĀ

An Examination of Agent and Object

1. An existing agent cannot generate an existing object and a non-existing agent cannot crave for a non-existing object.
2. That which exists has no action; therefore the object would be without an agent. An existing agent cannot have action; therefore an agent would be without an object.
3. If a non-existing agent were to create a non-existing object, then the object would be without a cause and the agent would not have caused anything either.
4. In the absence of a cause, effect and cause would not exist; in the absence of an effect and a cause action, agent and instrument would cease to be.
5. If action etc. are not possible, then there would be no *dharma* and *adharma*. In the absence of *dharma* and *adharma* the result arising from them would also not exist.
6. In the absence of the result, the path leading to emancipation or to heaven would have no justification. In this manner all actions would become meaningless.
7. An existing – non-existing agent cannot produce an existing- non-existing result, because existence and non-existence being opposed to each other, how could they belong to the same entity?
8. An existing agent cannot create a non-existing object and a non-existing agent cannot create an existing object. All those objections would arise in this case.
9. An existing agent cannot create a non-existing or an existing - non-existing object, because of the reasons stated earlier.

10. A non-existing agent cannot create an existing and an existing - non-existing object, because of the very reasons stated earlier.

11. An existing-non-existing agent cannot produce an existing-non-existing object. One should know this, because of the reasons stated earlier.

12. An agent is relative to an object and an object is relative to that very agent. We do not see any other reason establishing them.

13. In the light of the rejection of object and agent the rejection of material etc. also should be understood. On the pattern of object and the agent, remaining things should also be comprehended.

CHAPTER - IX

PŪRVA-PARĪKṢĀ

An Examination of Prior Existence

1. Some people say that the entity to which seeing, hearing etc. and feeling etc. belong, exists prior to them.

2. If that entity is non-existent, how would seeing etc. be related to that? Therefore the esistence of that entity prior to them is established.

3. (The Mādhyamikas answer by saying) Who knows the so-called existing entity established, being prior to seeing, hearing etc. and feeling etc.?

4. If that is established irrespective of seeing etc., then those seeing etc. also would, no doubt, exist without that entity.

5. An entity is manifested by something and something is manifested by another entity. Then, how could something exist without the other and how could the other things exist without that?

6. (The opponent says) There is nothing prior to the totalily of seeing etc. But at a time the one or the other among seeing etc. would be manifested.

7. (The Mādhyamikas say) If there is nothing prior to the totality of all the seeing etc., then how could one be prior to the other one individually?

8. He who sees is also the one who hears, and also the same has feeling, then one would be prior to the other. But this is not justified.

9. It the one who sees is different from the one who hears and the one who has feeling, then the one who hears would be possible only when there is an entity which sees, and thus there would be many souls.

10. The elements from which seeing, hearing etc. and feeling etc. proceed would have no souls in them.

11. It that entity to which seeing, hearing etc. and feeling etc. belong does not exist, then these also would not exist.

12. Nothing exists prior to seeing etc. or at the time of seeing etc. or after them. The imposition of the construction of existence and non-existence does not apply here.

CHAPTER X

AGNĪNDHANA-PARĪKṢĀ

An Examination of Fire and Fuel

1. If fuel be the same as fire, then the agent and the object would become one. If fire were different from fuel, then fire would be possible without fuel.

2. Fire would ever remain burning in the absence of the cause of burning. Again, attempt to rekindle fire would be futile, as fire would remain without object.

3. Because, one would not require the other, as it would be without the cause of burning, it would be constantly burning. Any attempt to rekindle it would be futile.

4. If fuel be that which is being burnt by fire, then by what would fuel be burnt if fuel be only that much (being burnt).

5. If fire be different from fuel, then it would not be in contact with fuel. Not being in contact with fuel, it would not burn. Again, if not burning, fire would not extinguish. If not extinguished it would remain with its mark.

6. If fire being different from fuel were to come in contact with fuel, it would be like a woman coming in contact with man and a man coming in contact with a woman.

7. Let fire which is different from fuel come in contact with fuel, if fire and fuel were to exclude each other.

8. If fire were to require fuel and fuel were to require fire, then which of the two is established first, in relation to which there would be fire or fuel.

9. If fire were relative to fuel, it would amount to establishing fire, what is already established. Also, this being the case fuel would be without fire.

10. The entity which is established depending upon something and the latter were to need the former, then that which is required to be established would be dependent upon the other. In this case which would require what?

11. The entity which is established depending upon something, being itself non-established, how should it require that something? If it having been established, requires the other, its requirement is not justified.

12. Fire does not exist depending upon fuel; fire does not exist not depending upon fuel. Fuel does not exist depending upon fire and fuel does not exist not depending upon fire.

13. Fire does not come from somewhere. Fire does not exist in fuel. The rest of the points here in this context of fuel, are the same as stated in the context of that which is being traversed, that which is already traversed and which is yet to be traversed.

14. Fuel is not the same as fire, nor does fire exist in anything other than fuel. Fire has no fuel; fuel does not exist in fire. Fire also does not exist in fuel.

15. The entire proceedings of soul and its material are fully explained, along with jar, cloth, ghaṭa, paṭa etc., by the discussion of fuel and fire.

16. Those who talk of things allied to soul and other entities separately, I consider them to be ignorant of the meaning of the teachings of the Buddha.

CHAPTER - XI

PŪRVĀPARAKOṬI-PARĪKṢĀ

An Examination of Prior and Posterior

1. The great sage said that the beginning point is not known. The series of birth-death (*saṃsāra*) is without beginning and end; it has no first and no last point.

2. That which is devoid of the beginning and the end, how could there be a middle point in it? Therefore, the order of the beginning, the end and the simultaneity cannot be justified in this case.

3. If, first, there be birth and thereafter decay and death, then birth would be without decay and death and a thing would be born not having died.

4. If there were decay and death in the beginning and birth afterwards, then how could there be, without a cause, decay and death of that which is not yet born?

5. It is not justified to say that birth exists along with decay and death. That which is being born would die at the same time and the two would be without a cause.

6. Where these beginning, end and simultaneity are not possible, why do they explain such birth and those decay and death?

7-8. Effect and cause, the thing characterized and the characterization, feeling and whofeels it — these and all those things that there could be, not only the series of birth-death, have no beginning point.

CHAPTER - XII

DUḤKHA-PARĪKṢĀ
An Examination of Suffering

1. Suffering is self-generated; it is generated by some other agency; it is generated by both, it is also without cause. These are the views of some thinkers. But suffering as a result cannot be justified.

2. If it were self-generated, it would not originate relative to those (dying) aggregates; as these (newly originating) aggregates originate relative to those (dying aggregates).

3. If depending aggregates were to be different from the aggregates depended upon and the aggregates depended upon were to be different from the depending aggregates, then alone suffering would be generated by some other; as it would then be created by others.

4. If suffering were created by one's own psychophysical organism (*pudgala*) then what kind of that psychophysical organism free from suffering, would be, which would itself create suffering?

5. If suffering be created by another psychophysical organism and having created it that other organism were to present it to someone, then how that receiving psychophysical organism be devoid of suffering?

6. If suffering were created by another psychophysical organism, then what kind of organism that would be which itself has no suffering but having created it would present that suffering to others?

7. If self-generated suffering is not established, how could that generated by others be possible? Because the other who creates suffering, that suffering would be his self-creation.

8. Suffering is not self-created, because the self does not create itself. If the other is not self-created, how could that other create suffering?

9. If suffering were to be created by each one of the two, then alone it would be said to have been created by both. How could there be that uncaused suffering which has not been created either by others or by oneself?

10. Not only suffering cannot have four kinds, external entities also cannot have four kinds.

CHAPTER - XIII

SAṂSKĀRA-PARĪKṢĀ

An Examination of Impressions

1. That which has borrowed characteristics is false - this is what the Buddha said. All the impressions have borrowed characteristics. Therefore, they are false.

2. If a thing having borrowed characteristics is false, what is it that is borrowed? This point has been stated by Lord Buddha by way of exposing the nature of *s'ūnyatā.*

3. Things have no identity (*svabhāva*) of their own because they are seen to become otherwise. There cannot be anything devoid of identity, as things have *s'ūnyatā.*

4. If there is no identity, what would become otherwise? If a thing has got its own identity, what would become otherwise?

5. The same thing cannot become otherwise, nor can another thing become otherwise. As a youngman cannot become old, and an old man cannot become old.

6. If the same thing can become otherwise, then milk itself would become curd. What else would become curd other than milk?

7. If there is something not *s'ūny*a, then some other thing would be *s'ūny*a. There is nothing which is not *s'ūn*ya. How could then something become *s'ūny*a?

8. The Buddha has said: *s'ūnyatā* consists in going away from all standpoints. Those who have *śunyatā* as a standpoint are declared by him to be incurable.

CHAPTER - XIV

SAṂASARGA-PARĪKṢĀ

An Examination of Connection

1. Among these three, viz., the object of cognition, cognition and the cogniser either any two or all the three cannot have connection with each other.

2. Attachment, he who has the attachment and the object of attachment are also to be similarly viewed. Remaining afflictions (*kles'ā*) and remaining bases (*āyatana*) are in this way considered by placing them under three divisions.

3. Connection of one is possible with the other, but that otherness of the object of cognition etc. is not possible. So they cannot have connection.

4. Not only the object of cognition etc. have no otherness, but anything in relation to any other thing cannot justifiably have otherness.

5. One relative to the other produces some other thing; without there being some other, the other cannot produce one other thing. That depending on the other produces another, but that other is not possible.

6. If that which depending on the other be taken to produce some other things without taking the other into consideration, then the other would not be possible without taking another into consideration. Therefore, the other does not exist.

7. Otherness does not exist in the other and also it does not exist in that which is not the other. In the absence of otherness, there is nothing other or the same.

8. One thing cannot have connection with itself and another thing cannot have connection with one other. Being in connection, the object of connection and the agent of connection are, therefore, not possible.

CHAPTER - XV

SVABHĀVA-PARĪKṢĀ

An Examination of Identity

1. Identity cannot justifiably be produced by causes and relativity. Identity produced by causes and relativity would become created.

2. How, then , identity be created? Because identity is non-artificial and independent of anything else.

3. In the absence of identity, how could there be otherness? As identity is said to be otherness of otherness.

4. Again, how could there be any existence other than identity and otherness? There being identity or otherness existence can be established.

5. If existence remains not established, absence cannot be established; because people say that absence is an existence existing otherwise.

6. Those who hold identity, otherness, existence and absence, do not see the essence underlying the teachings of the Buddha.

7. In the *Kātyāyanāvavāda Sūtra* the Buddha, while analysing existence and absence, has rejected both 'is' , and 'is not'.

8. If a thing has existence by nature, then its non- existence would not be possible; as nature can never justifiably become otherwise.

9. If the nature does not exist, what would become otherwise? If the nature exists, what will become otherwise?

10. To say 'It is' is to hold eternality; 'It is not' is to hold nihilistic view. Therefore, an intelligent man should not uphold existence and non-existence.

11. 'That which is by nature existent cannot become non-existent' this is eternality. 'It is non-existent at present but it existed earlier' -this is nihilism.

CHAPTER - XVI

BANDHAMOKṢA-PARĪKṢĀ

An Examination of Bondage and Liberation

1. If impressions are transitory, then they cannot be eternal, because they transit. They cannot be non-eternal as they transit. The same position holds in restpect of empirical selves (*sattva*).

2. If the psychophysical organism (*pudgala*) were to transit, then that organism, inspite of five-fold search, is not to be found among aggregates (*skandha*), bases (*āyatana*) and elements (*dhātu*). Then who will transit?

3. If it transits from one material (*upādāna*) to another material, then it will become deviod of existence, i.e. aggregates. Who will transit, being devoid of existence (aggregates) and having no material?

4. The cessation of impressions can in no way be justified. The cessation of empirical self can also in no way be justified.

5. The impressions, which are characterised by origination and destruction, cannot be bound and cannot be liberated. In the aforesaid manner the empirical self also cannot be bound and cannot be liberated.

6. If material be the bondage, then a thing having material would not be bound and a thing having no material would not be bound. In what state will that be bound?

7. Let bondage bind freely, provided bondage be having existence prior to that which is bound. But this does not obtain. The rest of the points have been said as in the case of that which is being traversed, that which is already traversed and that which is not yet traversed.

8. He who is bound cannot be released; he who is not bound cannot also be released. The person in bondage and the person released together will be bound or released simultaneously.

9. People who hold fast the view "being free from material I shall be released. I shall get released", have for themselves the great snare of material.

10. Where there is no imposition of *nirvāṇa* and no demotion of the birth-death cycle, what would there be the birth-death cycle and how would *nirvāṇa* be imagined?

CHAPTER - XVII

KARMA-PHALA-PARĪKṢĀ

An Examination of Action and Result

1. That mind is a characterizing element (*dharma*) which controls the self, is benevolent towards others and is friendly. It is the seed of the result here as well as in the world after death.

2. The great Sage has called that action to be consciousness and what is done after consciousness. That action has been stated to have many varieties.

3. That action which is called consciousness is recognised as mental. That which is done after consciousness is said to be bodily and vocal actions.

4-5. The following seven characterising elements (*dharmas*) are expressed by action viz., speech, movement, non- abstention, which are called unconscious, and other unconscious abstentions, merit accompanied by indulgence, as well as demerit of that kind and consciousness.

6. If action were to stay till the time it becomes ripe, then it would become eternal. If it were destroyed, then having been destroyed what result would it generate?

7. That process beginning with sprouting starts from the seed and then the result is obtained. Without the seed the process will not start.

8. The process is generated by seed and the result emerges from the process. Therefore, seed being at the root of every result, the result would be neither destroyed nor it would become eternal.

9. The process of mind which is generated by mind leads to the result. This process cannot start without there being mind.

10. Because the process is generated by mind and the result is obtained from this process, the result is thus preceded by action. Therefore, this result is neither destroyed, nor it is eternal.

11. There are ten paths of white acts which are the means of accomplishing characterising elements (*dharma*). There are five elements of enjoyments (*kāma-guṇa*) in this world and in the world after death, which are the results of this characterising element (*dharma*).

12. There are some who think that there would be many serious defects, if this view is accepted. Therefore, this view cannot be justified.

13. I will state that thinking which would be justified here. This thinking has been elaborated by the Buddhas, Pratyeka Buddhas and the S'rāvakas.

14. Just as by writing a loan deed the loan is not destroyed, similar is the non-destruction of action. It is of four kinds in accordance with the material and by nature it is not explicable.

15. It cannot be removed by the act of removal; it can only be removed by contemplation. Therefore, because of this non- destruction, actions create result.

16. If the non-destruction of action were to be destroyed by action or it were to be destroyed by the process of action, then the defect of destroying action etc. would be in order.

17. All the actions whether of different categories or of the same category, on conjoining with their elements, yield that one i.e., non-destruction.

18. This non-destruction in respect of all the two types of action arises for each action in this very existence, and continues to exist even after fruition.

19. It would be destroyed either by change in the result or by death. It would indicate the distinction of *sāsrava* and *anāsrava* action.

20. The Buddha has said that there is *s'ūnyatā*, but no destruction. There is the world but is not eternal. There is no destruction of action.

21. Why is action not produced? Because it has no identity of its own. Because it is not produced, it is not destroyed.

22. If action were to exist in its identity, then undoubtedly it would be eternal. Moreover, action would become non-created, as nothing eternal can be created.

23. There would be the fear of getting the result for action which is not done. If action were not created, there would also be the defect of uselessness of staying with the preceptor.

24. There is no doubt that all the transactions (*vyavahāra*) would be contradicted.. There would be no distinction between a sinner and a holy-man.

25. If action were to be in identity, it would stay as established and would again yield result inspite of its having already produced a result.

26. This action is of the nature of suffering. But sufferings are not real. If those sufferings are not real, how could action be real?

27. Action and suffering are said to be relative to bodies. If action and sufferings are *s'ūnya*, then what could be the fate of bodies?

28. An individual is enveloped in ignorance and is bound by the fetters of desire. He is an enjoyer, he is none other than the agent and he is no more the same as he has been.

29-30. This action is neither created in relativity, nor has it arisen outside relativity. But because this action is there, there is, because of the same reason, no agent. If there is no action and no agent, how could there be the result born of action? In the absence of the result, how could there be an enjoyer?

31-32. Just as the Buddha, by virtue of his spiritual power, were to create an artificial being and that artificial being in its turn were to create another artificial being, then that artificial agent and action done by him would also be artificial; it is like an artificial being artificially created by another artificial being.

33. Suffering, actions, bodies, agents and results have the from of a city appearing in the sky (*gandharvanagara*) and are like mirage and dream.

CHAPTER - XVIII

ĀTMA-PARĪKṢĀ

An Examination of Soul

1. If soul were an aggregate, it would be subect to origination and destruction. If it were differnt from aggregates, then it would be devoid of the characteristics of the aggregates.

2. If there is no-soul, how could there be things related to soul? In the event the soul and things related to the soul are overcome, a Yogin would be free from the sense of 'I' and 'mine'.

3. He who is free from the sense of 'I' and 'mine' also does not exist. He who finds that which is free from the sense of 'I' and 'mine' does not really find anything.

4. The sense of 'I' and 'mine' in respect of external and internal things having been destroyed, material (*upādāna*) is destroyed. Because of the destruction of material birth is destroyed.

5. As a result of the destruction of action and suffering, liberation is attained. Action and suffering owe existence to mental constructions (*vikalpa*). Mental contructions are the creations of the use of language. But the use of language stops in the realm of *s'ūnyatā*.

6. The Buddha said: 'There is a soul'; 'There is no-soul'; and also 'There is neither any soul nor no-soul'.

7. The obect we talk about does not exist. In the absence of any object of mind, the true nature of things (*dharmatā*) which neither originates, nor is destroyed, becomes *nirvāṇa*-like.

8. Everything is what it is; it is not what it is; it is both what it is and what it is not; and it is neither what it is and what it is not. This is the teaching of the Buddha.

9. The characteristic of the nature of a thing is that it cannot be expanded by the use of language; it is free from mental constructions and it is not differentiated *(a- nānārtha)*.

10. Everything that originates relatively does not remain the same; nor it becomes different. Therefore, it is neither destroyed, nor it remains the same for ever.

11. The nectar of the teachings of the Buddha, the Lord of the Universe, is that there is nothing unitary or manifold; there is no annihilation, nor eternal existence.

12. The knowledge of the Buddha in respect of non-origination, the knowledge of *s'rāvaka*s in respect of annihilation, and the knowledge of *Pratyeka* Buddha arise without any contact.

CHAPTER - XIX

KĀLA-PARĪKṢĀ

An Examination of Time

1. If the present and the future were relative to the past, then the present and the future would be possible in the past time.

2. If the present and the future are absent in the past, then how could the present and the future originate depending upon the past?

3. The two times cannot be established without their relativity to the past. Therefore, there is nothing like the present and the future time.

4. In this manner the remaining two aspects of time, as well as 'high', 'low', 'middle' etc. and 'one' etc. sould be characterized.

5. That time which is not stable cannot be comprehended but there is no stable time which could be comprehended. How could time not comprehended be talked about?

6. If time were relative to existense, how could there be time without existence? Since there is no existence, how would then time be possible?

CHAPTER - XX

SĀMAGRĪ-PARĪKṢĀ

An Examination of Totality of Causes

1. If a result is produced by the totality of causes and relativity, the result has to exist in that totality. How then can it be produced by that very totality ?

2. If a result is produced by the totality of causes and relativity, but the result does not exist in that totality, how can it then be produced by that very totality?

3. If a result exists in the totality of causes and relativity, it should be obtained in that totality. But it is not obtained.

4. If a result does not exist in the totality of causes and relativity, then the causes and relativity would become like non-causes and non-relativity.

5. If a cause, after contributing causality (hetukaṃ) ceases to be, then there would be two aspects of a cause: one which is contributed and the second, which ceases to be.

6. If a cause, not having made any contribution towards a result ceases to be and the result is produced after the destruction of the cause, then that result would be without a cause.

7. If a result were to come into being simultaneously with the totality, then that which produces and that which is produced would become simultaneous.

8. If a result were to come into being before the totality, then that result, being free from causes and relativity, would become without a cause.

9. If a result were to emerge after the cause ceases to be, then the cause would continue transiting. Because, the cause which was produced earlier, would again be reproduced.

10. How could a cause which ceased to be and, thus, is no

more, give rise to an already produced result? Even if a cause were to exist, how could it create, being associated with a result?

11. If it is not associated with the result, what result would it produce? A cause does not produce a result by perceiving or not perceiving it.

12. There is no connection whatsoever of a result which is no more with a cause which ceased to be or a cause which is not yet born or a cause which is presently born.

13. A result which is already produced cannot have any connection whatsoever with a cause which is not yet born, or with a cause which ceased to be or with a cause which is presently born.

14. A result which is not yet born cannot have any connection whatsoever with a cause which is presently born, or with a cause which is not yet born or with a cause which ceased to be.

15. In the absence of any connection, how could a cause produce a result? Or, even if there is a connection, how could a cause produce a result?

16. If a cause be disconnected with a result, how could it produce that result ? If a cause be not disconnected with a result, how could it produce the same?

17. A result is not produced without being disconnected. A result does not cease to be without being disconnected. Such a result which would not cease to be would not be produced and would not be disconnected.

18. How could a disconnected result be produced? How could a disconnected result cease to be? That which though is disconnected but does not cease to be would become not produced.

19. The oneness of a cause and a result can never be justified. Difference of a cause from a result can also never be justifed.

20. The oneness of a result and a cause would amount to the oneness of the producer and the produced. The difference of a result from a cause would mean the oneness of a cause with non-cause.

21. Which cause would produce a result existing in its identity? What cause would produce a result which does not have its identity?

22. That which does not produce cannot be justifiably a cause. If causality is not justified, to what would the result belong?

23. The totality of causes and relativity, if cannot produce itself by itself, how could that totality produce a result?

24. A result is neither a product of totality, nor it is a product of non-totality. How could the totality of relativity exist without a result?

CHAPTER XXI

SAMBHAVA-VIBHAVA-PARĪKṢĀ

An Examination of Emergence and Dissolution

1. Dissolution is not possible either with emergence or without emergence. Emergence is not possible either with or without dissolution.

2. How could dissolution be possible without emergence? In the absence of emergence, dissolution would be like death without birth.

3. How could dissolution be possible along with emergence? Because, birth and death cannot exist simultaneously.

4. How could emergence be possible without dissolution? It is not that impermanence is never absent in things.

5. How could emergence exist along with dissolutions, as birth and death cannot exist at the same time.

6. There are no two things whose existence could be established with the help of each other or without the help of each other. How would the two be established?

7. Destruction does not emerge; non-destruction also does not emerge. There is no dissolution of destruction and there is no dissolution of non-destruction.

8. Emergence and dissolution are not possible in the absence of existence. No existence is possible without emergence and dissolution.

9. Emergence and dissolution cannot justifiably belong to s'*ūnya*. Emergence and dissolution cannot justifiably belong to non-s'*ūnya*.

10. It is not justified to hold emergence and dissolution to be one. It is not justified to hold emergence and dissolution to be different.

11. The opponent may hold that emergence and dissolution are perceived. (It is said in reply that) Emergence and dissolution are perceived on account of delusion.

12. Existence cannot come out of existence. Existence cannot come out of non-existence. Non-existence cannot come out of non-existence. Non-existence cannot come out of existence.

13. Existence is not born of itself; nor it is born from the other. It is also not born both of itself and the other. How is it then born?

14. He who holds existence would have to hold eternalism or nihilism. That existence would be either eternal or non-eternal.

15. The opponent may hold that to him who accepts existence, there is neither nihilism nor eternalism. The series of emergence and dissolution of result and cause is what constitutes existence (bhava)

16. (The Mādhyamika says that) If the series of emergence and dissolution of result and cause be existence, then dissolution not emerging again would lead to the annihilation of cause.

17. A thing existing in its identity cannot justifiably become non-existent. Moreover, at the time of *nirvāṇa* the series of existing stops, as it is annihilated.

18. The last point in the series if destroyed, existence cannot be justifiably the first point (in the next series). If the last point in the series is not destroyed, existence cannot justifiably be the first point (in the next series).

19. If the last point having been destroyed, the first point in the next series emerges, then that which is destroyed would be one and that which emerges would become another.

20. That which is being destroyed cannot be justified to have emergence again. If destruction and emergence are simultaneous, then it would emerge in the same aggregate where it was destroyed.

21. In this way the series of existence is not in order in all the three times. That which does not exist in all the three times how could that be the series of existence?

CHAPTER XXII

TATHĀGATA-PARĪKṢĀ

An Examination of Tathāgata

1. *Tathāgata* is not the aggregates. He is not different from the aggregates. He does not exist in the aggregates. The aggregates do not exist in him. He does not possess the aggregates. Then which one of these is *Tathāgata*?

2. It the Buddha does not exist in his identity depending upon the aggregates, then how could that which does not exist in identity be existing otherwise?

3. That which is relative to others is justifiably not the essence (*ātman*). How could that which is non-essence be *Tathāgata*?

4. If a thing does not exist in identity, how can it exist by virtue of something else? Who could that be Tathāgata without existing in identity or not having the nature of the other?

5. (The opponent says) If there be any *Tathāgata* not relative to the aggregates, he may now be relative and may exist relatively.

6. (The Mādhyamika says) There is no *Tathāgata*, not being relative to the aggregates. That which does not exist in relativity, how could that be relative to others?

7. There is nothing like relativity which is not relative. In no way Tathāgata is without relativity.

8. After searching for him in five ways as the same or the other etc. if not found, how could that kind of *Tathāgata* be talked about in terms of relativity?

9. That which is the object of relativity does not exist in identity. What does not exist in identity, how can that exist by virtue of others?

10. In this way relativity and the one who depends on it are totally *s'ūnya*. How can a *s'ūnya Tathāgata* be talked about by means of *s'ūnya*?

11. One should not call him *s'ūnya* or not-*s'ūnya* or both or neither. He is talked about only for the sake of the use of language.

12. How could four categories of eternality, non-eternlity etc. be applicable to him who is quiet? How could four categories of having end, having no end etc. be applicable to that which is quiet?

13. He who holds fast the view that *Tathāgata* exists or does not exist indulges in mental constructions about the one who has attained *nirvāṇa*.

14. In respect of the Buddha whose identity is *s'ūnya*, it is not justified to think whether the Buddha exists or does not exist after *nirvāṇa*

15. All of them who use language to describe the Buddha, who is beyond language and is without change, are afflicted by linguistic use and do not see *Tathāgata*.

16. What is the identity of *Tathāgata* is also the identity of this world. *Tathāgata* is without identity, so is this world without identity.

CHAPTER XXIII

VIPARYĀSA-PARĪKṢĀ

An Examination of Perversion

1. Attachment, aversion and delusion are said to be caused by resolution (*saṃkalpa*). They originate relative to goodness, badness and perversion (respectively).

2. Those which originate being relative to goodness, badness and perversion are in identity non-existent. Therefore, afflictions are not real.

3. Existence and non-existence of soul can in no way be established. Without that soul how could existence and non- existence of afflictions be established.

4. These afflictions happen to someone, but that someone is not established. Something may exist without another thing, but afflictions do not belong to someone.

5. Afflictions, like the view of one's own body, have no existence in all the five ways in that which is afflicted. The thing afflicted also, like the view of one's own body, does not exist in all the five ways in afflictions.

6. Goodness, badness and perversions do not exist in their identity. What goodness, badness and perversion would afflictions be relative to?

7. Form, sound, taste, touch, smell and mental object, these are six things which are imagined to be the objects of attachment, aversion and delusion.

8. Isolated form, sound, taste, touch, smell and mental objects have the form of *gāndharvanagara* and are like mirage and dream.

9. How would badness or goodness belong to those which are like an illusory person and like reflections?

10. We say that there is no goodness which does not depend upon badness. Being relative goodness cannot be justified.

11. We say that there is no badness which does not depend upon goodness. Being relative badness cannot be justified.

12. How could there be attachment when there is no goodness? How could there be aversion when there is no badness?

13. If holding that which is non-eternal to be eternal be perversion, then there being no non-eternal in *s'ūnya*, how could holding that way be perversion?

14. If holding that which is non-eternal to be eternal be perversion, then why not holding non-eternal in respect of *s'ūnya* be perversion?

15. The means of holding, holding, he who holds and that which is held - all these are quiet. Therefore, there is no holding.

16. In the absence of holding anything as true or false, to whom shall perversion or non-perversion belong?

17-18. There is no perversion in respect of the person who is already perverted. No perversion is possible also in respect of persons who are not perverted. No perversion is possible in respect of a person who is in the process of being perverted. Think yourself to whom will perversion possibly belong.

19. How could such perversions be possible which are not yet born? When perversions are not born, how could someone be in perversion?

20. A thing is not born by itself. It is not born from something other. Nor it is born by itself and from other. How could then there be someone in perversion?

21. If pure, eternal and blissful soul exists, then the soul is pure, eternal and blissful and there is no perversion.

22. If pure, eternal and blissful soul does not exist then impure, non-eternal no-soul being there, suffering would not be possible.

23. Thus, as perversion ceases to exist, ignorance ceases to exist. Ignorance ceasing impressions etc. also cease to be.

24. If there are any afflictions in identity belonging to someone how could then they be removed? Who can discard identity?

25. If any afflictions having identity do not exist in someone, how could then they be removed? Who can discard non-existents?

CHAPTER XXIV

ĀRYASATYA-PARĪKṢĀ

An Examination of Noble-Truths

The view of the opponent :

1. If all this is *s'ūnya*, there would be no origination and no destruction. There would be the absence of four noble truths for you.

2. In the absence of four noble truths, knowledge, removal, contemplation and realization would not be possible.

3. In the absence of that, there would be no four noble results. In the absence of the results, there would be no person inclined to the result.

4. If for you (the Mādhyamika) there would be no eight kinds of persons, then there would be no *Saṃgha*. In the absence of four noble truths there would be no *saddharma*.

5. In the absence of dharma and *Saṃgha*, how could there be the Buddha? Speking thus you are denying all the Three Jewels.

6. You by holding *s'ūnyatā* are denying the existence of results, good and bad deeds, as well as all the worldly transactions.

The Mādhyamika replies:

7. On this we say that you do not know the purpose of *s'ūnyatā, s'ūnyatā* and the meaning of *s'ūnyatā*. This is the reason why you are beating yourself.

8. The teaching of dharma by the Buddha takes into account two truths: the truth of worldly covering (*saṃvṛti*) and the ultimate truth (*paramārtha*).

9. Those who do not know the distinction between these two truths, they do not know the deep essence of the teachings of the Buddha.

10. The ultimate truth cannot be proclaimed without taking into account the worldly transactions. Without knowing the ultimate truth, *nirvāṇa* cannot be attained.

11. *S'ūnyatā,* if not known properly, destroys the person of feeble mind, like a serpent, not held properly, or a science not cultivated in the right manner.

12. This is the reason why realizing that persons of feeble mind would find it difficult to fathom this *dharma*, the

Buddha held back his mind from teaching the truth.

13. Moreover, the objections you raise regarding *s'ūnyatā*, do not affect us, as the same do not apply to that which is *s'ūnya*.

14. To the persons to whom *s'ūnyatā* is consistent, everything is consistent. To the person to whom *s'ūnya* is not consistent, everything becomes in-consistent.

15. By throwing your own faults on us, you are forgetting the very horse you are riding.

16. If you perceive the truth existing in identity, then in this way you are perceiving things without causes and relativity.

17. You are denying effect, cause, agent, the means, action, origination, destruction and the result.

18. What is relative origination is called by us *s'ūnyatā*. That *s'ūnyatā* consists in the use of language in relation to things. The same is also called the Middle Path.

19. There is nothing which is not relatively originated. This being so, there is nothing which is not *s'ūnya*.

20. If all this is not *s'ūnya*, there is no origination and no destruction. For you (the opponent) there will be the absence of four Noble Truths.

21. How could there be suffering which is not relatively originated? If it has identity, then suffering, which is said to be non-eternal, would not be possible.

22. What will originate again, if it were to exist in identity? Therefore, to the person who denies *s'ūnyatā*, there is no emergence.

23. Suffering, if existing in identity, cannot be destroyed. By holding identity of a thing you are contradicting its destruction.

24. There being identity, the contemplation of the path cannot be justified. If the path is contemplated upon, then for you it would have no identity.

25. When suffering, emergence and destruction have no existence, then on account of the cessation of suffering, which path would lead to it ?

26. If it is not known having identity, how could its knowledge be possible ? because identity would always be there.

27. Like knowledge, its removal, realization, contemplation and four noble results would not be possible.

28. If you hold that there is identity, how could the result not comprehended in identity be subsequently comprehended?

29. In the absence of result, there would be no persons attaining that result. If those eight persons do not exist, the *Saṃgha* cannot exist.

30. Because of the absence of Noble Truths, there would be no dharma. In the absence of dharma and *Saṃgha,* how could there be the Buddha?

31. For you the Buddha would be possible even without being relative to the *Bodhi* (Supreme Enlightenment). The *Bodhi* would also become possible without being relative to the Buddha.

32. He who is not a Buddha in identity, would not, according to you, obtain *Bodhi* even though he might exert along the path of Bodhisattva for attaining knowledge.

33. No one would ever do good or bad deeds. What is that which no-*s'ūnya* could do, as identity cannot be created.

34. For you there would be the result without good or bad deeds. For you there would be no result created by good or bad deeds.

35. If for you there were a result created by good or bad deeds, then how could the result generated by good or bad deed be non-*s'ūnya*?

36. If you are denying *s'ūnyatā* to relative origination, you are denying all the worldly transactions.

37. If you are denying *s'ūnyatā*, there would be nothing to be done; action would never start and there would be an agent not acting.

38. If identity is accepted, then the world would become unborn, non-destroyed, static and devoid of all the multi-faceted states.

39. If there is no *s'ūnya*, then it would not be possible to obtain something which is not yet obtained; there would be no action leading to the cessation of suffering and there would be no removal of all the afflictions.

40. He who sees relative origination, sees the following: suffering, emergence, cessation and the path.

CHAPTER XXV

NIRVĀṆA-PARĪKṢĀ

An Examination of Nirvaṇa

1. (It is said:) If it is all *śūnya*, there would be no origination, no destruction; by virtue of the removal or cessation of which whose nirvāṇa would be desired?

2. (The Mādhyamika says) If it is all not *śūnya*, there would be no origination, no destruction, by virtue of the removal or cessation of which whose nirvāṇa would be desired?

3. Not removed, not obtained, not destroyed, not eternal, beyond cessation and not originated - this is what is called nirvāṇa.

4. Nirvāṇa is not existent, as it would be characterised by decay and death. Without decay and death existence would not be possible.

5. If nirvāṇa be existent, then nirvāṇa would be a composite entity (*saṃskṛta*). Nowhere there is any entity which is non-composite (*asaṃskṛta*).

6. If nirvāṇa be existent, how could it be not relative? There is nothing existing which is not relative.

7. If nirvāṇa is not existent, how could nirvāṇa be non-existent? Where there is no existence, non-existence does not necessarily obtain.

8. If nirvāṇa be non-existent, how could then nirvāṇa be not relative? As there is no non-existence which is not relative.

9. That very coming and going which is dependent or relative is called nirvāṇa, when it is viewed having no dependence and relativity.

10. The Master taught the removal of birth and death. Therefore, it is proper to say that nirvāṇa is neither existence nor non-existence.

11. If nirvāṇa were both existent, and non-existent, then liberation also would be existent and non-existent - which is not proper.

12. If nirvāṇa were both existent and non-existent, then nirvāṇa would be not without dependence, as both these are also dependent.

13. How could nirvāṇa be both existent, and non-existent, as nirvāṇa is non-composite (*asaṃskṛta*) and existence and non- existence are composite (*saṃskṛta*) entities.

14. How could both existence and non-existence be possible in nirvāṇa? They cannot exist together like light and darkness.

15. The admission that nirvāṇa is neither existent, nor non-existent, can be substantiated only when

non-existence and existence are established.

16. If nirvāṇa is neither non-existent, nor existent, then who would conceive that it is neither non-existent, nor existent?

17. It cannot be thought that the Buddha exists after nirvāṇa. Similarly, it cannot also be thought that he does not exist, he is both, and is neither.

18. One cannot even say that the Buddha exists, even though he may be present. Similarly, it cannot also be thought that he does not exist, or he is both, or is neither.

19. There is no speciality of the world distinct from nirvāṇa. There is no speciality of nirvāṇa, distinct from the world.

20. There is not even the minutest difference between the category of nirvāṇa and the category of the world.

21. After cessation the view of end etc. and eternality etc. are dependent upon nirvāṇa, being at the last point and at the first point.

22-23. When all the things are *s'ūnya*, what is without end, what is that which ends? What is that which is both without end and with end; what is that which is neither with end nor without end? What is the same, what is different; what is eternal, what is non-eternal? What is both eternal and non- eternal? What is none of the two?

24. The Buddha has nowhere, to nobody, taught any truth which is the cessation of all objectivity, cessation of speech and is the Good.

CHAPTER XXVI

DVĀDASAṄGA-PARĪKṢĀ

An Examination of Twelve Links

1. A person covered by the ignorance of three kinds, augments those impressions for being reborn, whereby goes to the appropriate world by means of actions.

2. In the next birth consciousness enters relative to impressions. In the entering consciousness name and from are sown.

3. In the name and form which are sown there arise six bases (*āyatana*). In accordance with the six bases contact arises.

4. Conciousness acts relative to eyes, form, their conglomeration, name and form.

5. That where form, consciousness and eyes -these three, converge is called contact. From that contact arises feeling.

6. Craving arises relative to feeling, because a person craves in accordance with feeling. A craving person takes up four kinds of material (*upādāna*).

7. There being material, disposition to be born (*bhava*) arises in the person having material. If a person has no material he would be liberated and there would be no disposition for rebirth.

8-9. Five aggregates make disposition. From this disposition arises birth. Old age, death, suffering, grief along with crying, apprehensive mind and painful effort arise from birth. In this way the aggregates of only suffering arise.

10. An ignorant person, therefore, augments the impressions rooted in the world. Therefore, an ignorant person is the agent, not a wise person, because he perceives the truth.

11. When ignorance is arrested, the impressions do not arise. Arresting the ignorance is possible by means of knowledge, coupled with meditation alone upon it.

12. By arresting one, other does not arise. In this way this aggregate of only suffering is properly arrested.

CHAPTER XXVII

DṚṢṬI-PARĪKṢĀ

An Examination of View-Points

1. 'I was in the past', 'I was not in the past',: these and views about eternal existence etc. have concern with a previous existence.

2. 'I shall not be in the future', 'What else shall I be' these and views about termination etc. have concern with an existence hereafter.

3. 'I was in the past', - this is not justified. He who was in former birth is not the same as the one in the present.

4. (The opponent may say that) Though the soul remains the same, only its material (*upādāna*) becomes distinct. (In reply the Mādhyamika asks) What would be the soul, distinct from material to you?

5. If it is said that there is no soul, free from the material, then the material itself would become the soul. For you, then, there would be no soul.

6. Material is not the soul, because it originates and dies. How could he who receives material be the material itself?

7. The soul being different from material is not justified. If it is without material and different from it, it could be found in that form; but it is not so found.

8. In this way, the soul is neither different from material, nor it is the material itself. The soul is not without material, nor it is decided that there is no soul.

9. 'I did not exist in the past': this cannot be justified. The person in the present cannot be different from the person existing in past births.

10. If the present person were to be different, then it would exist inspite of past births. He would exist in the same manner, or he would be born not having died.

11. There would be annihilation, destruction of actions and the enjoyment of action done by others etc.

12. It cannot also be said that he is born without existing previously. There would be objections. The soul would be either created or it would be born without a cause.

13. In the same way, the views concerning the past, viz. 'I was not there', 'I was there', 'I was both and neither' are not justified.

14. Concerning the future, the view 'Whether I shall be or shall not be' is similar to the views concerning the past.

15. 'He was a god, and the same became a man': This would be eternalism. A god should exist without birth, as an eternal person is not born.

16. 'Man is different from god', this would be a view of non-eternality. If a man be differnt from god, then there would be no continuity.

17. If a part were godly, and a part humnaly, then he would be both eternal and non-eternal. This is not justified.

18. If a thing were both eternal and non-eternal, then it has to be established, otherwise it would be neither eternal, nor non-eternal.

19. If something were to come from somewhere, and then it were to go somewhere, then the world would become beginningless. But it is not so.

20. If there is nothing eternal, who would be non-eternal? Being both eternal and non-eternal is rejected by these two.

21. If this world were to have an end, then how would there be the world hereafter? Again, if this world were to be without an end, could there be a world hereafter?

22. This continuity of aggregates is, since, like the flame of a lamp, it cannot be justified to have an end nor no end.

23. If the former aggregates were destroyed and subsequent aggregates were not to be born, relative to these aggregates, then, the world would be with an end.

24. If the former aggregates were not destroyed, and the latter aggregates were not to be born, relative to these aggregates, then, this world would be without an end.

25. If a part were to have an end, the other part were to have no end, then the world would be both with and without an end, - which is not justified.

26. How could one part of a person be destroyed and the other part not destroyed? Thus, it is not justified.

27. How could one part of the material be destroyed and another part be not destroyed? This is also not justified.

28. If both having an end and not having an end were to be established, it would not have an end nor would it have no end.

29. Or, because of all things being *s'ūnya,* how many views like eternalism etc. would arise and from what source, to whom, and where?

30. He who taught *saddharma* out of compassion, with a view to removing all the views, I bow to that Gautama.

EXPLANATORY NOTES

CHAPTER I

PRATYAYA-PARĪKṢĀ

1-2 These two *Kārikās* briefly state that the subject-matter of the *Madhayamaka-S'āstra* is the relative origination having eight characteristics. Its aim is to obtain *nirvāṇa,* where all linguistic descriptions terminate.

No-cessation : Cessation means the termination of a moment.

No-origination : Origination means emergence of a thing.

No-annihilation : Annihilation means the termination of the series of moments.

One-thing : One thing means a thing not differentiated.

Relative Origination : This is the translation of the original word '*Pratītyasamutpāda*'. '*Pratītya*' is a combination of the prefix '*prati*' and the verbroot '*iṇ*', which means movement. The complex word '*pratītya*' therefore means reaching and relation. '*Samutpāda*' is emergence. The total expression means origination of a thing in relation to causes and condition.

According to some '*pratītya*' means a thing destroyed repeatedly.

Termination of linguistic description: This is the translation of the word '*prapañca*'. In the Mādhyamika philosophy language ramifies a thing described.

3. According to Buddhapālita things do not originate themselves, because it is useless that thing existing by itself would originate again. Bhāvaviveka criticises this position by saying that no reason has been given in support of this view. Candrakīrti does not agree with

Bhāvaviveka by saying that there is no use of free inference in the Mādhyamika system, because it does not admit any position which could be accepted or rejected. It only negates the position held by others. Thus for the Mādhyamika the use of inference is in the context of the view held by others, in order to show the inherent defect in the reasoning of others. This is what is called contextual use of inference (*prasaṅga anumāna*).

According to Candrakīrti the eight adjectives, like origination etc., are in order only to an ignorant person. The person free from ignorance has an object for his knowledge which is free from all these adjectives. Nāgārjuna wrote this work in order to show the illusory character of all the objects. An ordinary man takes everything true as it appears to him. Here this apparent character is denied and a thing is shown to be illusory in its apparent form. He who knows illusory character of things does not entertain its existence or non-existence in its apparent form.

According to Candrakīrti the statement of the Buddha like 'Impressions originate on the basis of ignorance' is only an apparent statement, having no truth. According to him, in all appearance there is an awareness of reference. The cause and the result are relative to each other and to the object of reference therefore are included under appearance. They have no identity of their own. 'This being, that arises' is only an indicative statement, having no truth behind it. Causation etc. are rooted only in linguistic usage. One cannot assert causation to be the identity of a thing. All usages are relative, whereas identity of a thing is non-relative. Therefore, it is proper to understand the entire *Madhyamaka-S'āstra* as a critique of different linguistic usages. Here Nāgārjuna has shown that any philosophical position has no connection whatsoever with the identity of a thing.

4. The four conditions are as follows:

Cause It is that condition which makes a thing.

Support : It is the condition on the basis of which something originates.

Non-mediation : That which without any mediation originates an effect e.g. the cessation of a cause is the immediate condition for the origination of an effect.

Predominant : Predominant condition is that the being of which makes emergence possible, as e.g. there being seed, sprout emerges.

'There is no fifth condition' means that God etc. are not accepted as a condition.

5. In any one of the four conditions mentioned above an effect cannot have its identity. Identity means a thing's own nature. It is only through its own nature that a thing is identified.

6. There is no relation between the act of change and relativity. Though they are not separate still they together are considered in out ordinary experience.

7. 'Why is it not no-relativity?' means that indeed it is no-relativity.

10. Those who believe support to be a relativity hold that a thing exists without any support first, but accepts support subsequently. It is pointed out in criticism that if a thing could remain first without any support, then why would it need support afterwards.

12. This is the criticism of a predominant condition. Cause and effect do not form the identity of the thing. Therefore, to say 'this being, that exists' cannot be proved.

CHAPTER - II

GATĀGATA-PARĪKṢĀ

1. The idea here is that traversing feet are made of atoms. The atom behind the tip of the finger has been traversed and the atom in front is not yet traversed; there being no atom inbetween which is being treversed. Here the question of the relation of an atom to four directions would lead to breaking of atom in parts, as Vasubandhu has said in the *Vijñaptimātratāsiddhi* (Viṃs'atikā, Kārikā-12)

2. This *kārikā* contains the view of the opponent attempting to prove the existence of the path being traversed at present.

3. The view of the opponent is refuted here and the Mādhyamika position is stated.

   Two traversings - The act of trversing is present in two: traversing in the path being traversed and traversing in the person traversing. In reality there is only one traversing act. Therefore, to say that the path is being traversed is not justified because there is no second traversing in the path.

4. If the act of traversing is supposed to be in the path then the path being only the locus of the act will be devoid of its own traversing act. Without there being the act of traversing the use of the verb 'to traverse' would not be justified.

8. The idea that one who goes does not go, will be clarified in subsequent three *kārikās*.

9. In the statement 'The goer goes', there is only one act of going. How can he who does not go become a goer? If this in not possible how the act of going be available in

two places, i.e. in the goer and in going?

10. The idea in this *kārikā* differs from the one stated in the previous *kārikā*. The previous *kārikā* shows that the statement 'Goer goes' is not justified. In the present *kārikā*, however, the expression 'goer' would signify the act of going. Therefore, to add further 'is going' would be redundant.

13. If a person is static then in relation to him the path traversed and the path not yet traversed cannot be referred to. That which has not yet been traversed has no relation with the past act, nor is it connected with the present act. Therefore, in that context the talk of going is inconsistent.

15. This *kārikā* is a reply to the attempt made by the opponent to justify the possibility of the opposite of the act of going. For example, if there is light, its opposite, darkness, would be possible; or if there is doubt then there would be the possibility of its opposite. Staying is the opposite of going; therefore, going is possible. The idea contained in the expression 'The goer does not stay' is elucidated in the sixteenth *kārikā*. 'Non-goer does not stay' means that the non-goer is very much staying. The concept of non-going contains the idea of staying. Therefore, the statement 'Non-goer is staying' refers to the state of staying twice.

17. This *kārikā* assumes the view of the opponent that since going starts, there is the act of going. When the act of going ends, the state of staying begins. To this Nāgārjuna says that the goer cannot be dissociated from the path being traversed; as has been said that the path being traversed is not possible. In the same way the path already traversed and the path not yet traversed cannot also be said to be dissociated from the goer. The paths have no connection with the act of going.

18-19. The 19th *kārikā* explains what has been said in 18th *kārikā*.

22. Before a person starts going, he cannot be called a goer. Therefore, the goer does not exist prior to the act of going. Similarly, only when there is some place to go, different from the goer, then the goer goes there. There is no existence of a goer prior to the act of going. A person not connected with the act of going cannot go anywhere. Therefore, it is said, 'Someone goes some place'.

24-25. There are three possibilities - (1) the goer is existent and is associated with the act of going, (2) the goer is non-existent and is not associated with the act of going, and (3) it can be existent as well as non-existent. Similarly, the act of going is also possibly of three kinds. The idea is that the existing goer cannot be associated with existing, non-existing, and existing-non-existing act of going. This will be explained in detail in the chapter *karmakāraka-parīkṣā.*

CHAPTER III

CAKṢURĀDĪNDRIYA-PARĪKṢĀ

1. This *kārikā* presents the view of *Abhidharma*, to the effect that seeing etc. are there by nature. The Mādhyamika denies this and holds that they are not natural, because seeing takes place with the help of eyes but its object is a form. Moreover, seeing does not see itself. Therefore, this cannot be the nature of one who sees.

3. This *kārikā* presupposes the following view of the opponent and provides a rejoinder to that. The view of the opponent is that just as fire does not burn itself, but

it burns something different from itself, in the same way seeing does not see itself but only others. In short, the answer to that view is that the thing already burnt is not being burnt; the thing which is not yet burnt is not being burnt. In the same way that which has been already seen is not being seen and that which is not yet seen is not being seen. The thing being seen has no existence apart from having been seen and not yet seen.

5. 'The seeing sees' is a statement which assumes relation of the act of seeing either with the eyes having the nature of seeing or with the eyes without that nature. The answer given here amounts to saying that in case the eyes have the nature of seeing, then 'The eyes see' would be a repetition of seeing. Then seeing should take place twice. If, on the other hand, eyes are devoid of the nature of seeing, then they cannot be related to the act of seeing.

   According to the *Sautrāntikas* seeing is not an act. It is only a state of affairs. Therefore, since there is no act of seeing, 'Seeing does not see' is a justifiable statement. Candrakīrti holds against the above view of the *Sautrāntikas* that there can never be a state of affairs without action. Every state of affairs has to be active. It may also be pointed out that if there is no act possible, no state of affairs would also be possible.

6. There is no seer apart from seeing. If this is not so, he who does not see would also be called a seer.

7. The view of the *Vaibhāṣika* is stated in this *kārikā*.

8. The view presented in the previous *kārikā* is being refuted here.

9. The remaining bases (*āyatanas*) are rejected on the line of the refutation of seeing.

CHAPER IV

SKANDHA-PARĪKṢĀ

1. Form (*rūpa*) is physical and is caused by four great elements (earth, water, fire and air). There is no form available apart from these elements.

2. When a form already exists, then it does not need any cause. When a form does not exist then whose cause would be sought?

3. The view of the opponent to which this *kārikā* provides an answer is that there being a form there must be a cause of it. Nāgārjuna's answer to this is that the form cannot be an effect, because it has already been shown that there is no cause of form.

4. The cause of form would be anything solid or liquid, hot or cold material element, but the form is not that. Again, if the effect and cause are not similar then the two would be incompatible.

8. in debate the rejection of the view of the opponent is attempted. The form has been shown to be without identity; with the help of *s'ūnyatā* the identity view is rejected. The opponent holding the identity view may refute the Mādhyamika view by saying that just as there are feeling etc., in the same way there is form also. This rejoinder would not be proper, because feeling etc. are to be proved, just as form is to be proved. Any attempt made by any non-Mādhy mika philosopher would in this way amount to saying what is yet to be proved. The Mādhyamika holding *s'ūnyavāda* can never commit this logical fallacy.

9. The act of exposition consists in the explanation of the Mādhyamika position to an inquisitive student. The student may raise some points for seeking some clarification against the Mādhyamika position. The objection of the student would have the same status as

given in the previous *kārikā.*

CHAPTER V

DHĀTU-PARĪKṢĀ

1. There are six basic elements (*dhātus*) viz. earth, water, fire, air, *ākās'a* and consciousness. In the present chapter *ākās'a* is being examined with a view to reject all the basic elements. According to the *Vaibhāṣ'ika-ākās'a* is characterized as the absence of cover. The question is whether *ākās'a* exists before this characterization or not? If it does not exist, then there is nothing which could be characterized. If, on the other hand, there is a thing existing prior to characterization and characterization is applied to it afterwards then characterization would become meaningless.

   Here 'characterisation' means that linguistic description of the conglomeration of qualities whereby the identity of a thing could be established. In this chapter Nāgārjuna criticises those views which hold that the identity of a thing is known through its characterisation.

3. That which is without characterisation would be without identity and therefore non-existent. No characterisation would be possible of a thing which does not exist. There is no entity which is with or without characteristics. These are mutually exclusive and jointly exhaustive. Therefore, being contradictory,both of them reject any attempt of characterisation.

6. If there be an existing entity it could be characterized but it has been shown that characterisation is not possible. The opponent therefore proposes that if *ākās'a* is not an existing entity let it be a non-existing entity. The present *kārikā* states that non-existence is always relative to existence. If *ākās'a* be not an existing entity, then it could also not be a non-existing entity.

Moreover, if *ākās'a* be conceived as non-existence of form etc. then we have to establish that form etc. which could have existence.

Similarly, a knower would also be either an existing or a non-existing person. Such a person having the characterization of knowing would have therefore to be established as is the case with *ākās'a.*

8. *'Good which is the quitessence of all that could be perceived'*: that which is free from all the imaginations of knower, known, characterisation etc. is called the Good, which is the ultimate truth. All characterizations are ramifications of language. *S'ūnyatā* consists in getting free from this ramification.

CHAPTER VI

RĀGARAKTA-PARĪKṢĀ

1. Attachment is one of the sufferings. Only when there is a person with attachment, he will suffer on account of attachment. The Buddha has talked about the suffering of the person with attachment. Therefore, there has to be a person before he gets attachment. This view has been criticised in the present *kārikā.* A person free from attachment cannot be said to be with attachment. Otherwise an *Arhat* would also become afflicted with attachment.

3. This *kārikā* shows that there would be the fallacy of independence, if there is no relation of temporal sequence between attachment and the person having attachment.

8. If the opponent were to hold that though attachment and the person with attachment cannot be established independent of each other, still they may co-exist, then the answer is that their togetherness could be established only when they are established separately.

CHAPTER VII

SAṂSKṚTA-PARĪKṢĀ

1. A thing which is subject to origination, destruction and change is called *saṃskṛta*, which is the subject matter of examination in this Chapter. The question is whether origination itself is *saṃskṛta* or *asaṃskṛta* ? if it is *saṁskṛta* it must have all the three characteristics mentioned above.

4. According to the *Sāmmitīya* School of Buddhism origination also originates and there is no defect of infinite regress. A *saṃskṛta* element originates along with fourteen other elements viz. the originating element, its origination, the process of its coming into being, its existence, decay and impermanence; its painfulness, goodness, its capacity to lead or not to lead to *nirvāṇa*. This is called the original or the first origination. The origination of origination comes later. The original origination causes the origination of fourteen elements and the origination of origination causes the origination of the original origination. Hance no infinite regress.

14. In the first thirteen *kārikās* it is established that origination is not because of origination of itself. In the present *kārikā* the point being established is that origination cannot originate others. As is stated in the second chapter, existence being originated is not possible because there is no third possibility beyond the originated and the non-originated. Again, that which is already originated is not being originated, as there is a contradiction between the past and the present. That thing is called originated wherein the act of origination is exausted. Similarly, the thing being originated is so-called wherein the act of origination is continuing. In the statement, 'The originated thing is being originated', there would be simultaneity of the past and the present.

Likewise, if that which is not yet originated is supposed to be being originated, then there would be contradiction between the future and the present. Hence, the view that origination originates another thing is not justified.

15. The opponent may say that only when there is origination, depending upon that the thing being originated would be established. The thing being originated is the result of the act of origination. This view of the opponent is controverted in the present *kārikā*. In order to justify the statement 'A thing being originated orginates, relative to origination', we have to determine the thing being originated. But this is not possible because for determining there must exist the thing being determined. The thing being originated is not available for determination.

16. An existing thing must have its identity and should not depend upon origination etc. This is the view of the philosopher who upholds identity view. On this basis there would be no scope for origination in relativity. According to the philosopher holding the relational origination view both cause and effect would be quiet i.e. without identity.

17. If a thing prior to its origination were to exist, not having been originated, then alone it would be considered originating, depending upon the act of origination. But prior to origination non-originated thing is not possible. What would then originate?

Candrakīrti raises an interesting point in the form of the following view of the supposed opponent. Though a thing called 'jar' does not exist prior to its origination, even then one can say that the thing to be originated would be called 'jar'. Candrakirti reacts to this by saying that the thing coming into existence would be called 'jar' only when the act of origination starts. But that which is still in the future cannot be an object of the process of origination. How could then such a thing be the object of the act of origination and thus be called present? If it is said that the act of origination proceeds in respect of something non-jar, then we have to clarify what in meant by 'non-jar.' Would this non-jar be a cloth or would it be nothing? If it were cloth in the state of non-origination, how could it be called 'jar' when originated ? If it is nothing, then how could the act of origination proceed in respect of such a thing which is nothing and how could that nothing become jar? Therefore, the name to be given to a future thing cannot establish origination.

22. The examination of the *saṃskṛta* element called existence starts from here. A thing which exists cannot have the act of existence because existence emerges only when the act stops.

26. From here starts the examination the *saṃskṛta* elements called impermanence.

28. If the thing has the form of milk, then the form of curd cannot be the cause of destruction of the form of milk. Since milk and curd do not exist simultaneously, the form of curd cannot destroy the form of milk.

30. Destruction means absence. That which is destroyed does non exist. Therefore destruction of an existing thing would mean the presence of existence and non-existence together in the same thing. Both of them being contradictory, nothing would be either existent or non-existent.

31. Nobody has two heads. Therefore, cutting of the second head would be like the destruction of non-existence.

32. Here the main point of discussion is whether the cessation of cessation is possible. Candrakīrti holds against those who do not accept the possibility of cessation of cessation, that cessation would not be *saṃskṛta* if it were not to cease. Therefore, our ordinary behaviour is the only basis for worldly life. Momentariness also would not be natural to a thing. It has to depend upon origination.

CHAPTER VIII

KARMAKĀRAKA-PARĪKṢĀ

2. An existent agent cannot create an existing object :

7. Existing-non-existing agent cannot create an existing non-existing object.

12. The agent and the object have mutual dependence. They are thus dependent upon each other.

13. Like mutual dependence of agents and objects the accepted material thing also is being rejected. Mutual dependence is not natural because both lack identity.

CHAPTER IX

PŪRVA-PARĪKṢĀ

1-2. It has been said in the thirteenth *kārikā* of the last chapter that there is no one to hold seeing etc. together. According to the view of the *Sāmmitīya* school something like a soul is needed. This view has been expressed in the first two *kārikās* of this chapter.

6. This also is the view of the *Sāmmitīyas*.

8. If the same person were to be the seer, heares etc. then even without the act of seeing a hearer may be called a seer. Such a view is controverted here by holding that for each activity there is a distinct agent.

11. Candrakīrti raises a question : is it definite that there is no soul In answer he says "Who said that there is no soul" ? He further elaborates that an existing soul posited by imagination has no identity. The statement of the Mādhyamika aims at removing commitment to the identity of soul. This does not mean that the Mādhyamika

imagines soul to be non-existent. We have to get rid of commitment to both existence and non-existence of soul.

CHAPTER X

AGNĪNDHANA-PARĪKṢĀ

1. Here with the help of the example of fuel and fire the view of those philosophers who believe in the soul, holding together different modes of mental act, is being examined. The opponent may say that even a relative entity has identity; as for example fire is relative to fuel but fire has got identity in terms of its burning quality and fuel, likewise, though relative to fire, has its own identity. Similarly various mental acts are required for a soul and mental acts themselves require the soul. Therefore, both the soul and mental acts have identity. This is the view of the opponent which is being examined in the following *kārikās*.

13. Candrakīrti while commenting on this *kārikā* rejects the *Sāṃkhya* theory of prior existence of effect in a cause. If it is held that fire is latent in the stick and the same is manifest, then the question is asked: Whether this manifestation itself existed prior to manifestation?

15. *Upādāna* means five aggregates. What is true of soul is also true with regard to any entity like jar etc.

CHAPTER XI

PŪRVĀPARAKOṬI-PARĪKṢĀ

1. The opponent thinks that in the absence of a soul there would be no entity to fall in the cycle of birth and death. The statement of the Buddha on this question shows that there is the world of the cycle of birth and death and thus there has to be a soul in it. The entire chapter tries to show that there is no possibility of such a world.

CHAPTER XII

DUḤKHA-PARĪKṢĀ

1. The view of the opponent is that since there is suffering, it must belong to a soul. The present chapter rejects the possibility of suffering itself.

CHAPTER XIII

SAṂSKĀRA-PARĪKṢĀ

1. That which has characteristics taken from others is relatively originated, having no identity of its own. All the impressions are relatively originated.

2. The question is that if everything is false what could be borrowed from it? The answer is that falsity does not mean absence; it means being free from identity.

3. It is said that there is no entity devoid of identity and all entities are said to be *s'ūnya*. Thus the identity of any entity would be *s'ūnyatā*. In answer to this it is stated here that *s'ūnyatā* is the universal characteristic of all entities, therefore no entity devoid of *s'ūnyatā* is possible. When there is nothing, i.e. non-*s'ūnyatā*, its contradictory, *s'ūnyatā* is also not possible.

4. Going out of all standpoints does not mean any entity. Candrakīrti illustrates this point with the help of an example: Somebody says 'I have nothing in my possession to give'. Still a person may persist to have the 'nothing' itself. Those who have a standpoint about *s'ūnyatā*, they consider that nothing to be something.

CHAPTER XV

SVABHĀVA-PARĪKṢĀ

1. According to Nāgārjuna identity has to be necessarily a permanent feature. That which is caused cannot be the identity of a thing. Being caused and identity are mutually contradictory concepts.

2. Candrakīrti in his commentary explains that identity is the natural feature of a thing, which does not vary in all the three times; that which not being earlier is not created later; that which is not dependent upon causes and relativity and that which does not derive its characteristics being in relation to other things, like long and short etc. According to the Mādhyamikas this kind of identity is called *dharmatā* and *sūnyatā*. Such an identity can never be caused. Therefore, identitilessness is the real identity or suchness of a thing. Identity has been conceived as unborn. Therefore, the identity of *Tathatā* is really identitilessness.

6. The sayings of the Buddha are considered to be the source of knowledge. The sayings of the Buddha are taken to be āgama by Candrakīrti. According to him *āgama* is that which comes down from those trustworthy persons who are free from all the defects. *Āgama* is also so-called because it reveals truth in its entirety. According to the third interpretation *āgama* is that which having been revealed leads people through its force to *nirvāṇa*. All these three characteristics are present only in the sayings of the Buddha. Statements from others being devoid of these characteristics are not trustworthy. They are pseudo-*āgamas*.

9. Here the first question is the objection and the second question is a counter question, implying the answer.

11. The Mādhyamika accepts identitilessness. Therefore, both the view-points of eternality and nihilism are not possible

Candrakīrti raises an objection in the form of the view of an opponent, saying that he is a nihilist who denies identity to things. In answer he states that the philosophy of identitilessness is not a nihilistic philosophy. Had there been identity earlier and subsequently that were to be denied, then alone it would have become rightly a form of nihilism. A person suffering from *timira* disease in the eyes perceives floating hairs but the person free from that disease in that context says 'There is nothing'. The statement 'There is nothing' does not negate anything; it only states a fact of anything being not present there. From this point of view identitilessness is not nihilism.

CHAPTER XVI

BANDHAMOKṢA-PARĪKṢĀ

1 Eternal impressions cannot change, as that would involve contradiction. Transitory impressions would cease to exist because as soon as they are born they are destroyed.

If impressions were supposed to continue in a series, then they have to remember that which is produced does not come from anywhere, nor does it go anywhere. Transitory things, therefore, cannot really transit. If it is held that the previous moment transits to the following moment, then the two moments would become one; but being related as cause and effect, they cannot be one. Moreover, in case they are held to be one, then they cannot be prior or posterior. The destruction of the previous moment and the emergence of the following moment would also not be possible if the two moments were identical. On the other hand, if the two moments are different, then also there would be no transition of one to the other, as that would also involve the transition of *Arhat*. Thus, no moment can follow a moment which is destroyed, not destroyed or is in the process of destruction. In the theory of momentariness transition is not in order.

3. That which is devoid of aggregates has no cause but nothing can remain without a cause. A soul being thus without existence cannot change.

4. Both eternal and non-eternal impressions cannot achieve cessation. If *nirvāṇa* were to belong to that soul which cannot be described as eternal or non-eternal, then we have to accept the existing of soul in *nirvāṇa*. Moreover, since soul is described as eternal and non-eternal it cannot be without description.

8. A thing in bondage is not a free thing, because there is a contradiction in saying 'A thing in bondage is released'.

10. Both *nirvāṇa* and the world are imagined and as such there would be simple imposition of the imagined. Both these being without identity and being *s'ūnya* are one.

CHAPTER XVII

KARMAPHALA-PARĪKṢĀ

1. The first twenty *kārikās* of this chapter state the views of non-Mākhyamika Buddhist thinkers concerning the nature of the result of action. From *kārikā* twenty-one onward the Mādhyamika view is explained.

Ātman or soul is the locus in which egoism arises. Mind and consciousness determine the capacity of giving result in respect of good and bad actions. The mind controls the soul in respect of objects and determines efforts. The mind thus controlling the soul is called good and prevents it from killing etc. This is *dharma*-mind. The word '*dharma*' has three meanings : that which has its own characteristics; that which prevents from going to evil state and that which prevents going towards the world of five kinds. All the *sāsrava* and *anāsrava dharmas* belong to the first category, good dharmas belong to the second category and *nirvāṇa* is the *dharma* of the third category. In the present *kārikā* the *dharma* of the second category is meant.

In addition to the *dharma* controlling the soul benevolence towards others is also called a *dharma*. Thus, there are three kinds of *dharmas* referred to here.

2. Two types of *dharma* are mentioned here viz. consciousness and action done after consciousness. In subsequent three *kārikās* its various kinds are explained.

The Buddha is called the 'great sage' because he has realised the ultimate truth or the form of everything (*sarvākārajñatā*).

4-5. Speech of good or bad nature gives rise to consciousness which may be abstention or not abstention. So also is the case with the bodily movement. The conscious act is also of two kinds; one which communicates and the other which does not communicate consciousness to other. Non- communicating consciousness is also of two types; abstention and non-abstention.

Indulgence means using a thing given in charity.

7. This is in reply to the question raised in the previous *kārikā*.

8-9. The example of seed is for the explanation of the process of mind.

11. In the previous ten *kārikās* ten kinds of action are explained in order to clarify the nature of ten white acts. These are as follows: three kinds of act done by body,

four acts done by speech and three acts done by mind.

12. In this the view of another school of Buddhism is mentioned and what has been stated in previous eleven *kārikās* is being criticized.

According to Candrakīrti the main defect is as follows: the example of seed implies that like-effect is caused by only like-cause. Good act will generate only a good act. Man is generated by man and so on, but this is not so, because men and gods are supposed to move in many bodies according to good or bad acts.

13. This statement is on behalf of the school mentioned in the previous *kārikā*.

14. According to the explanation of Candrakīrti a good act is destroyed immediately after it is done but its result will persist, because along with the emergence of act a characteristic called *non-destruction* also arises in the agent, like a loan-deed. This loan-deed like non-destruction is bound to give result of its action to the agent. But once the loan-deed is encashed, it becomes infructuous so far as the subsequent attempt to encash is made. Therefore, the emergence of the result of an action is explained with the help of non-destruction characteristics.

According to the material (*dhātu*) this is of four types - *kāma, rūpa, arūpa and anāsrava.*

20. The view given here is an explanation of the statement of the Buddha as given by a non-Mādhyamika Buddhist school.

21. From here starts the exposition of the Mādhyamika view.

23. Staying with the preceptor for meditation leading to the attainment of *nirvāṇa.*

28. This is the view of an opponent.

29-30 This is the Mādhyamika position which amounts to holding that the result of action also is non-real. This point is further explained in subsequent three *kārikās*.

CHAPTER XVIII

ĀTMA-PARĪKṢĀ

1. In his commentary on this *kārikā* Candrakīrti says that in the Brahmanical philosophy of *Sāṃkhya* etc. there is a different conception of soul viz. it is eternal, non-active, enjoyer, without characteristics and static. Candrakīrti responds to this view of soul by saying that the characteristics of soul mentioned above are not derived from direct perception of soul; they are based upon the traditions handed down.

2. Things related to soul are five aggregates.

3. He who is free from the sense of 'I' and 'mine' is a Yogin. Yogin also has no identity.

6. Sayings of the Buddha differ on account of different mental levels of the people to whom they are addressed. In an alternative explaination of this *kārikā* Candrakīrti identifies the view that there is a soul, to the position of *Sāṃkhya* and that there is no soul is the view of *Lokāyata*. The view of the Buddha is that there is neither any soul nor no soul.

7. This *kārikā* represents the gist of the teachings of the Buddha. That which is neither originated nor destroyed cannot be ta'`.ed about by means of language.

Candrakīrti raises a question that the view of the Mādhyamika, that there is no identity, is not materially different from the view of the nihilist. In reply he draws a distincation between *s'ūnyatā* and non-existence. For the Mādhyamika soul being relationally originated is not non-existent. He clarifies this point with the help of an example. A person has committed theft. One person not having seen him stealing accuses him of theft because of enimity. Another person accuses him of theft after actually seeing him stealing. The statement of both these person is true, so far as the act of stealing is concerned. But the first one speaks a lie and the second person speaks the truth. The Mādhyamika after knowing that things have no identity call them identitiless but the nihilist without knowing the truth calls them non-existent. Therefore, from the point of view of knowledge there is nothing common between the nihilist and the Mādhyamikas.

9. The characteristics of the nature of a thing given here also do not describe the true nature of a thing. It is also based upon workability. Language is a kind of ramification of the object it describes and thus it expands without justification, on the basis of the active mind which is called *vikalpa.*

12. There is no contact between a body, a mind and an object. *Pratyeka Buddha* knows about things without such a contact.

CHAPTER XIX

KĀLA-PARĪKṢĀ

1. Time is related to the identity of things. Do the present and the future times depend upon the past or do they not depend upon it? There dependence upon the past is not possible because for dependence the past must have existence in the present. But the past is non-existence. The view that the past contains within it the present and the future cannot be accepted because in the absence of the past the present and the future will also become absent. If the present and the future are absent, how would a thing have its past?

3. Those who believe that time is absolute are criticised by Nāgārjuna by saying that absolute time will not have the division of present, future etc.

4. Two aspects of time mentioned here are to be considered in the light of the first aspect, as discussed in the *kārikās* where it is said that the present and the future depend upon the past. In one of the aspects mentioned in this *kārikā* time is conceived with the present at the centre. In the second aspect the centre is occupied by the future. In all the three cases time being not possible, existence of a thing in time cannot be proved.

   According to the explanation given by Candrakīrti the first 'etc.' includes all the things dependent upon tripartite relations, like good-bad-indeferent; orgination- existence-destruction; anterior-prterior- middle etc. The second 'etc'. includes two, many etc. These are to be explained on the line of the explanation of three times.

5. This *kārikā* examines time conceived as moment, second, minutes etc.

6. This *kārikā* takes into account the concept of time as dependent upon the form etc. of things.

CHAPTER XX

SĀMAGRĪ-PARĪKṢĀ

1. Totality of causes and conditions means accessory causes.

2. According to the *Sāṃkhya-kārikā* things though existing cannot be perceived because of their minuteness etc. In such a case the existence of unperceived things is proved by means of inference etc. The Mādhyamika holds that both existence and non-existence of the result cannot be proved by means of inference. Therefore, the result cannot be included under totality. Candrakīrti says that the Mādhyamika is opposed to both existence and non-existence of the result. It only aims at the rejection of existence and non- existence as convceived by others.

8. This *kārikā* responds to the opponent Sāṃkhya view that the result exists in unmanifest form and the same is brought out into the present as a result of the operation of causes and relativity.

9. The cause itself transforms into the result - this is the view of *Sāṃkhya* to which the present *kārikā* responds. The transition of cause into effect means that no new effect is produced; rather the eternal cause is transformed into the result. When in reality the result is existing in the form of cause, then the talk of the production of the result is futile. 'Cause' and 'effect' are only words which in the view of *Sāṃkhya* would have no real meaning.

CHAPTER XXI

SAṂBHAVA-VIBHAVA-PARĪKṢĀ

1. Dissolution and emergence take place in time. By showing the impossibility of both these their relation to time is also rejected.

17. Annihilation of the series of the world at the time of *nirvāṇa* would go against the saying of the Buddha. This is shown in next four *kārikās*.

CHAPTER XXII

TATHĀGATA-PARĪKṢĀ

1. The Buddha motivated by great campassion exerted with the help of means and wisdom (*upāya* and *prajñā*) to the good of the entire universe through numberless lives. On account of his compassionate involvement for the good of others he attained omnisience, of the nature of the complete knowledge of all the forms of all the existing things. Thus he was called *Tathāgata* in the sense that he knew (*gata*) the things in the form in which they are (*tathā*). The opponent would raise an objection here that since one cannot become Tathāgata in one life there would have been a beginningless series of life. The existence of *Tathāgata* guartantees real cycle of birth and death. In reply the *Mādhyamika* says that had there been a person having the identity of *Tathāgata*, the cycle of birth and death could be established. But no such person is available with his own identity as *Tathāgata*. It is only under the influence of ignorance that the people talk of the identity of *Tathāgata*. This is what the present chapter tries to show.

2. The second *kārikā* provides an answer to the supposed view of the opponent that the Buddha depends upon pure aggreegates. But then such a Buddha is not possible.

CHAPTER XXIII

VIPARYĀSA-PARĪKṢĀ

4. The one to whom afflictions relate is the ground or locus which must exist prior to afflictions. Those who believe in soul consider the soul to be the locus of afflictions, as they happen to the soul. The Mādhyamika, who does not hold existence or non-existence of the soul, asks that there being no-soul what will be the locus of afflictions?

5. One's own body is the aggragate of form etc. Those who hold one's own body to be the soul hold the view that affliction etc, happen to the afflicted mind. On the line of the five-fold rejection of the identification of *Tathāgata* with the aggregates (as given in *kārikā* 22.1) the view concerning form etc. to be the basis of afflictions should also be rejected. Thus, there cannot be any afflicted mind as the locus of afflictions.

7. A thing is said to be the locus of attachment etc. According to Candrakīrti there are six kinds of things as the locus of form etc. Form is the basis on which a thing is identified as existing here or there. Sound is that which sounds or reveals an object. Smell is that which arrests a thing. Taste is the object which is tasted. Touch is the object of touching. A mental object is that which has generic and specific characteristics. These six kinds of things are the locus of afflictions. When a thing is imagined to be good it gives rise to attachment. When a thing is imagined to be bad it creates aversion. When a thing is imagined to be eternal soul etc. would create delusion. Thus attachment, aversion and delusion being imposed on things by mind are imagined.

13. There are four kinds of perversion -

i) To consider momentary aggregates as eternal;

ii) Non-eternal is suffering but to consider suffering aggregates to be pleasant;

iii) The body is always in all respects sinful. To condider this to be good;

iv) Five aggregates have the characteristics of non-endurance, origination and destruction and devoid of permanence. Thus, being contrary to the character of soul, to consider the aggregates as soul these four kinds of perversions create delusion.

The eternal being the opposite of non-eternal, how could it be a perversion, when there is no non-eternal? Thus all the perversions are rejected.

15. Quiet means not being born. In identity a thing is like *nirvāṇa*

CHAPTER XXIV

ĀRYASATYA-PARĪKṢĀ

1. Four truths are called Noble Truths because only noble or enlightened people know them as truth after the removal of all kinds of delusions.

4. *Saddharma* is the way good people live.

7. The purpose of *s'ūnyatā* is the quietitude of all language. *S'ūnyatā* means transcendence of language. The meaning of *s'ūnyatā* is origination in relativity as it will be explained in *kārikā* 18 of this chapter.

8. *The truth of worldly covering;* in the Mādhyamika philosophy 'world' means what is known as a living being depending upon five aggregated. 'Covering' means that which covers all around the true nature of all the entities.

According to another interpretation 'covering' means mutual dependence. The third interpretation is the linguistic usage on which our worldly transaction depends. That which appears to be true on account of this worldly covering, but is not really true, is called 'the truth of worldly covering'.

10. The Buddha talked about things like aggregate etc. This is not the ultimate truth. Only because on the basis of inferior truth he wanted to proclaim the ultimate truth.

11. The use of language is possible because it describes a whole, consisting of parts. A thing is conceived as a whole in language but this whole is not born in identity. This is what is called *s'ūnyatā* or the Middle path.

CHAPTER XXV

NIRVĀṆA-PARĪKṢĀ

1-2 The first *kārikā* represents the view of the opponent to which the second *kārikā* provides an answer.

3. *Nirvāṇa* does not increase or decrease like attachment. It cannot be obtained, as the result of *śramaṇahood* is obtained. It is not destroyed like aggregates. According to the *Mādhyamika* since there exists nothing in identity prior to *nirvāṇa,* nothing is destroyed when *nirvāṇa* is obtained.

8. Whenever *nirvāṇa* is called non-existent it only means the absence of existence i.e. the rejection of imagined existence.

21. There are four possible views regarding what happens after *nirvāṇa* viz. *Tathagāta* exists after death, he does not exist, he both exists and does not exist and he neither exists nor does not exist.

The view of end etc. are four - the universe has an end, it has no end, it is with and without end and it is neither with nor without end. These are related to the *nirvāṇa* being the last point. The following four views relate to *nirvāṇa* being the first point, viz., universe is eternal, ot non-eternal, it is both eternal and non-eternal, it is neither eternal nor non-eternal.

CHAPTER XXVI

DVĀDAŚĀṄGA-PARĪKṢĀ

1. There are three kinds of impressions: goods, bad, indifferent. According to another interpretation three kinds of impressions relate to body, speech and mind.

2. The next birth in the form of god, man etc. contains consciousness generated by impressions. This consciousness inspires the self.

Name is that which forces consciousness to move to different bodies. According to another interpretation a name is that which by virtue of being a sign leads to an object. A form is that which is comprehended or which is contradicted.

In his commentary on this *kārikā* Candrakīriti refutes the idea of momentary entity in detail. His basic argument is that an entity which exists just for one moment cannot contain origination and destruction together.

6. Four *upādānas* or materials are desire, view-point, conduct and attachment to a soul.

CHAPTER XXVII

DṚṢṬI-PARĪKṢĀ

1. There are eight views relating to a previous existence.

These are as follows - 'I was in the past', 'I was not in tha past', 'I was and I was not in the past', 'Neither I was nor I was not in the past'. Likewise the world is eternal, not eternal, both eternal and non-eternal, neither eternal, nor non-eternal.

2. Existence hereafter means existence which is to come after the present one. These are also of eight types: 'I shall be', 'I shall not be', 'I shall and I shall not be', 'Neither I shall be, nor I shall not be in the future'. 'This world is terminal', 'not terminal', 'is and is not terminal', 'neither is, nor is not terminal'.

NĀGĀRJUNA
MADHYAMAKA-ŚĀSTRAM

I

PRATYAYA-PARĪKṢĀ

anirodham anutpādam anucchedam as'ās'vatam |
anekārtham anānārtham anāgamam anirgamam || 1

yaḥ pratītya -samutpādaṃ prapañcopas'amaṃ s'ivm |
des'ayāmāsa sambuddhas taṃ vande vadataṃ varam || 2

na svato nāpi parato na dvābhyāṃ nāpy ahetutaḥ |
utpannā jātu vidyante bhāvāḥ kva cana ke cana || 3

catvāraḥ pratyayā hetur ālambanam anantaram |
tathaivādhipateyaṃ ca pratyayo nāsti pañcamaḥ || 4

na hi svabhāvo bhāvānāṃ pratyayādiṣu vidyate |
avidyamāne svabhāve parabhāvo na vidyate || 5

kriyā na pratyayavatī nāpratyayavatī kriyā |
pratyayā nākriyāvantaḥ kriyāvantas' ca santy uta || 6

utpadyate pratītyemān itīme pratyayāḥ kila |
yāvan notpadyata ime tāvan nāpratyayāḥ katham || 7

naivāsato naiva sataḥ pratyayo 'rthasya yujyate |
asataḥ pratyayaḥ kasya satas' ca pratyayena kim || 8

na san nāsan na sadasan dharmo nirvartate yadā |
kathaṃ nirvartako hetur evaṃ sati hi yujyate || 9

anālambana evāyaṃ san dharma upadis'yate |
athānālambane dharme kuta ālambanaṃ punaḥ || 10

anutpanneṣu dharmeṣu nirodho nopapadyate |
nānantaram ato yuktaṃ nirudhhe pratyayas' ca kaḥ || 11

bhāvānāṃ niḥsvabhāvānāṃ na sattā vidyate yataḥ |
satīdam asmin bhavatīty etan naivopapadyate || 12

na ca vyastasamasteṣu pratyayeṣv asti tat phalam |
pratyayebhyaḥ kathaṃ tac ca bhaven na pratyayeṣu yat || 13

athāsad api tat tebhyaḥ pratyayebhyaḥ pravartate |
apratyayebhyo'pi kasmāt phalaṃ nābhipravartate || 14

phalaṃ ca pratyayamayaṃ pratyayās' cāsvayaṃmayāḥ |
phalaṁ asvamayebhyo yat tat pratyayamayaṁ katham || 15

tasmān na pratyayamayaṃ nāpratyayamayaṃ phalam |
saṃvidyate phalābhāvāt pratyayāpratyayāḥ kutaḥ || 16

II

GATĀGATA-PARĪKṢĀ

gataṃ na gamyate tāvad agataṃ naiva gamyate |
gatāgatavinirmuktaṃ gamyamānaṁ na gamyate || 1

ceṣṭā yatra gatis tatra gamyamāne ca sā yataḥ |
na gate nāgate ceṣṭā gamyamāne gatis tataḥ || 2

gamyamānasya gamanaṁ kathaṃ nāmopapatsyate |
gamyamāneṃ dvigamanaṃ yadā naivopapadyate || 3

gaṃyamānasya gamanaṃ yasya tasya prasajyate |
ṛte gater gamyamānaṃ gamyamānaṃ hi gamyate || 4

gamyamānasya gamane prasaktaṃ gamanadvayam |
yena tad gamyamānaṃ ca yac cātra gamanaṃ punaḥ || 5

dvau gantārau prasajyete prasakte gamanadvaye |
gantāram hi tiraskṛtya gamanaṃ nopapadyate || 6

gantāraṃ cet tiraskṛtya gamanaṃ nopapadyate |
gamane 'sati gantātha kuta eva bhaviṣyati || 7

gantā na gacchati tāvad agantā naiva gacchati |
anyo gantur agantuś ca kas tṛtīyo hi gacchati || 8

gantā tāvad gacchatīti katham evopapatsyate |
gamanena vinā gantā yadā naivopapadyate || 9

pakṣo gantā gacchatīti yasya tasya prasajyate |
gamanena vinā gantā gantur gamanam icchataḥ || 10

gamane dve prasajyete gantā yady uta gacchati |
ganteti cocyate yena gantā san yac ca gacchati || 11

gate nārabhyate gantuṃ gantuṃ nārabhate'gate |
nārabhyate gamyamāne gantum ārabhyate kuha || 12

na pūrvaṃ gamanārambhād gamyamānaṃ na vā gatam |
yatrārabhyeta gamanam agate gamanaṃ kutaḥ || 13

gataṃ kiṃ gamyamānaṃ kiṃ agataṃ kiṃ vikalpyate |
adṛśyamāna ārambhe gamanasyaiva sarvathā || 14

gantā na tiṣṭhati tāvad agantā naiva tiṣṭhati |
anyo gantur agantuś ca kas tṛtīyo 'tha tiṣṭhati || 15

gantā tāvat tiṣṭhatīti katham evopapatsyate |
gamanena vinā gantā yadā naivopapadyate || 16

na tiṣṭhati gamyamānān na gatān nāgatād api |
gamanaṃ saṃpravṛttiś ca nivṛttiś ca gateḥ samā || 17

yad eva gamanaṃ gantā sa eveti na yujyate |
anya eva punar gantā gater iti na yujyate || 18

yad eva gamanaṃ gantā sa eva hi bhaved yadi |
ekībhāvaḥ prasajyeta kartuḥ karmaṇa eva ca || 19

anya eva punar gantā gater yadi vikalpyate |
gamanaṃ syād ṛte gantur gantā syād gamanād ṛte || 20

ekībhāvena vā siddhir nānābhāvena vā yayoḥ |
na vidyate tayoḥ siddhiḥ kathaṃ nu khalu vidyate || 21

gatyā yayocyate gantā gatiṃ tāṃ sa na gacchati |
yasmān na gatipūrvo 'sti kas'cid kiṁcid dhi gacchati || 22

gatyā yayocyate gantā tato 'nyāṃ sa na gacchati |
gatī dve nopapadyete yasmād eke pragacchati || 23

sadhbūto gamanaṃ gantā triprakāraṃ na gacchati |
nāsadbhūto 'pi gamanaṃ triprakāraṃ sa gacchati || 24

gamanaṃ sadasadbhūtaḥ triprakāraṁ na gacchati |
tasmād gatis' ca gantā ca gantavyaṃ ca na vidyate || 25

III

CAKṢURĀDI-INDRIYA-PARĪKṢĀ

dars'anaṃ s'ravaṇaṃ ghrāṇaṃ rasaṇaṃ spars'anaṃ manaḥ |
indrīyāṇi ṣaḍ eteṣāṃ draṣṭavyādīni gocaraḥ || 1

svam ātmānaṃ dars'anaṃ hi tat tam eva na pas'yati |
na pas'yati yad ātmānaṃ kathaṃ drakṣyati tat parān || 2

na paryāpto 'gnidṛṣṭānto dars'anasya prasiddhaye |
sadars'anaḥ sa pratyukto gamyamānagatāgataiḥ || 3

nāpas'yamānaṃ bhavati yadā kiṃ cana dars'anam |
dars'anaṁ pas'yatīty evaṁ katham etat tu yujyate || 4

pas'yati darśanaṃ naiva naiva pas'yaty adars'anam |
vyākhyāto dars'anenaiva draṣṭā cāpy upagamyatām || 5

tiraskṛtya draṣṭā nāsty atiraskṛtya ca darśanam |
draṣṭavyaṃ dars'anaṃ caiva draṣṭary asati te kutaḥ || 6

pratītya mātāpitarā yuathoktaḥ putrasambhavaḥ |
cakṣurūpe pratittyaivamukto vijāanasambhavaḥ || 7

draṣṭavyadars'anābhāvād vijñānādicatuṣṭayam |
nāstīty upādānādīni bhaviṣyanti punaḥ katham || 8

vyākhyātaṃ s'ravaṇaṃ ghrāṇaṃ rasanaṃ spars'anaṃ manaḥ |
darśanenaiva jānīyāc chrotrśrotavyakādi ca || 9

IV

SKANDHA-PARĪKSĀ

rūpakāraṇanirmuktaṁ na rūpam upalabhyate |
rūpeṇāpi na nirmuktaṃ dṛs'yate rūpakāraṇam || 1

rūpakāraṇanirmukte rūpe rūpaṁ prasajyate |
āhetukaṃ na cāsty arthaḥ kaśćid āhetukaḥ kva cit || 2

rūpeṇa tu vinirmuktaṃ yadi syād rūpakāraṇam |
akāryakaṁ kāraṇaṃ syād nāsty akāryaṃ ca kāraṇam || 3

rūpe saty eva rūpasya kāraṇaṃ nopapadyate |
rūpe 'saty eva rūpasya kāraṇaṃ nopapadyate || 4

niṣkāraṇaṁ punā rūpaṁ naiva naivopapadyate |
tasmād rūpagatān kāṃs'cin na vikalpān vikalpayet || 5

na kāraṇasya sadrs'aṁ kāryam ity upapadyate |
na kāraṇasyāsadṛs'aṃ kāryaṃ ity upapadyate || 6

vedanācittasaṃjñānāṃ saṃskārāṇāṃ ca sarvaśaḥ |
sarveṣām eva bhāvānāṃ rūpeṇaiva samaḥ kramaḥ || 7

vigrahe yaḥ parihāraṃ kṛte s'ūnyatayā vadet |
sarvaṃ tasyāparihṛtaṃ samaṁ sādhyena jāyate || 8

vyākhyāne ya upālambhaṃ kṛte śūnyatayā vadet |
sarvaṃ tasyānupālabdhaṃ samaṃ sādhyena jāyate || 9

V

DHĀTU-PARĪKṢĀ

nākās'aṃ vidyate kiṃcit pūrvam ākās'alakṣaṇāt |
alakṣaṇaṃ prasajyeta syāt pūrvaṃ yadi lakṣaṇāt || 1

alakṣaṇo na kas'cic ca bhāvaḥ saṃvidyate kva cit |
asaty alakṣaṇe bhāve kramatāṃ kuha lakṣaṇam || 2

nālakṣaṇe lakṣaṇasya pravṛttir na salakṣaṇe |
salakṣaṇālakṣaṇābhyāṃ nāpy anyatra pravartate || 3

lakṣaṇāsaṃpravṛttau ca na lakṣyam upapadyate |
lakṣyasyānupapattau ca lakṣaṇasyāpy asaṃbhavaḥ || 4

tasmān na vidyate lakṣyaṃ lakṣaṇaṃ naiva vidyate |
lakṣyalakṣaṇanirmukto naiva bhāvo 'pi vidyate || 5

avidyamāne bhāve ca kasyābhāvo bhaviṣyati |
bhāvābhāvavidharmā ca bhāvābhāvam avaiti kaḥ || 6

tasmān na bhāvo nābhāvo na lakṣyaṃ nāpi lakṣaṇam |
ākāśam ākāśasamā dhātavaḥ pañca ye pare || 7

astitvaṃ ye tu pas'yanti nāstitvaṃ cālpabuddhayaḥ |
bhāvānāṃ te na pas'yanti draṣṭavyopaśmaṃ śivam || 8

VI

RĀGA-RAKTA-PARĪKṢĀ

rāgād yadi bhavet pūrvaṃ rakto rāgatiraskṛtaḥ |
taṃ pratītya bhaved rāgo rakete rāgo bhavet sati || 1

rakte 'sati punā rāgaḥ kuta eva bhaviṣyati |
sati vāsati vā rāge rakte py eṣa samaḥ kramaḥ || 2

sahaiva punar udbhūtir na yuktā rāgaraktayoḥ |
bhavetāṃ rāgaraktau hi nirapekṣau parasparam || 3

naikatve sahabhāvo 'sti na tenaiva hi tat saha |
pṛthaktve sahabhāvo 'tha kuta eva bhaviṣyati || 4

ekatve sahabhāvas' cet syāt sahāyaṃ vināpi saḥ |
pṛthaktve sahabhāvas' cet syāt sahāyaṃ vināpi saḥ || 5

pṛthaktve sahabhāvas' ca yadi kiṃ rāgaraktayoḥ |
siddhaḥ pṛthakpṛthagbhāvaḥ sahabhāvo yatas tayoḥ || 6

siddhaḥ pṛthakpṛthagbhāvo yadi vā rāgaraktayoḥ |
sahabhāvaṃ kimarthaṃ tu parikalpayase tayoḥ || 7

pṛthag na sidhyatīty evaṁ sahabhāvaṃ vikāṅkṣasi |
sahabhāvaprasiddhyarthaṃ pṛthaktvaṃ bhūya icchasi || 8

pṛthagbhāvāprasiddhes' ca sahabhāvo na sidhyati |
katamasmin pṛthagbhāve sahabhāvaṁ satīcchasi || 9

evaṃ raktena rāgasya sidhir na saha nāsaha |
rāgavat sarvadharmāṇāṃ siddhir na saha nāsaha || 10

VII

SAṂSKṚTA-PARĪKṢĀ

yadi saṃskṛta utpādas tatra yukatā trilakṣaṇī |
athāsaṃskṛta utpādaḥ kathaṃ saṁskṛtalakṣaṇam || 1

utpādādyās trayo vyastā nālaṁ lakṣaṇakarmaṇi |
saṃskṛtasya samastāḥ syur ekatra katham ekadā || 2

utpādasthitibhaṅgānām anyat saṃskṛtalakṣaṇam |
asti ced anavasthaivaṁ nāsti cet te na saṁskṛtāḥ || 3

utpādotpāda utpādo mūlotpādasya kevalam |
utpādotpādam utpādo maulo janayate punaḥ || 4

utpādotpāda utpādo mūlotpādasya te yadi |
maulenājanitas taṃ te sa kathaṃ janayiṣyati || 5

sa te maulena janito maulaṁ janayate yadi |
maulaḥ sa tenājanitas tam utpādayate katham || 6

ayam utpadyamāns te kāmam utpādayed imam |
yadīmam utpādayitum ajātaḥ s'aknuyād ayam || 7

pradīpaḥ svaparātmānau samprakās'ayitā yathā |
utpādaḥ svaparātmānāv ubhāv utpādayet tathā || 8

pradīpe nāndhakāro 'sti yatra cāsau pratiṣṭhitaḥ |
kiṃ prakās'ayate dīpaḥ prākas'o hi tamovadhaḥ || 9

katham utpadyamānena pradīpena tamo hatam |
notpadyamāno hi tamaḥ pradīpaḥ prāpnute yadā || 10

aprāpyaiva pradīpena yadi vā nihataṃ tamaḥ |
ihasthaḥ sarvalokasthaṃ sa tamo nihaniṣyati || 11

pradīpaḥ svaparātmānau saṁprakās'ayate yadi
tamo 'pi svaparātmānau chādayiṣyaty asaṁśayam 12

anutpanno 'yam utpādaḥ svātmānaṃ janayet katham |
athotpanno janayate jāte kiṁ janyate punaḥ || 13

notpadyamānaṁ notpannaṃ nānutpannaṁ kathaṁ cana |
utpadyate tad ākhyātaṃ gamyamānagatāgataiḥ || 14

utpadyamānam utpattāv idaṃ na kramate yadā |
katham utpadyamānaṃ tu pratītyotpattim ucyate || 15

pratītya yad yad bhavati tat tac chāntaṃ svabhāvataḥ |
tasmād utpadyamānaṃ ca śāntam utpattir eva ca || 16

yadi kaścid anutpanno bhāvaḥ saṃvidyate kva cit |
utpadyeta sa kiṃ tasmin bhāva utpadyate 'sati || 17

utpadyamānaṃ utpādo yadi cotpādayaty ayam |
utpādayet tam utpādam utpādaḥ katamaḥ punaḥ | 18

anya utpādayati enaṃ yady utpādo 'navasthitiḥ |
athānutpāda utpannaḥ sarvam utpadyate tathā || 19

sataś ca tāvad utpattir asataś ca na yujyate |
na sataś cāsataś ceti pūrvam evopapāditam || 20

nirudhyamānasyotpattir na bhāvasyopapadyate |
yaś cānirudhyamānas tu sa bhāvo nopapadyate || 21

na sthitas tiṣṭhate bhāvo' sthito bhāvo na tiṣṭhati |
na tiṣṭhate tiṣṭhamānaḥ ko' nutpannaś ca tiṣṭhati || 22

sthitir nirudhyamānasya na bhāvasyopapadyate |
yaś cānirudhyamānas tu sa bhāvo nopapadyate || 23

jarāmaraṇadharmeṣu sarvabhāveṣu sarvadā |
tiṣṭhanti katame bhāvā ye jarāmaraṇam vinā || 24

sthityānyayā sthiteḥ sthānaṃ tayaiva ca na yujyate |
utpādasya yathotpādo nātmanā na parātmanā || 25

nirudhyate nāniruddhaṃ na niruddhaṃ nirudhyate |
tathā nirudhyamānaṃ ca kim ajātaṃ nirudhyate || 26

sthitasya tāvad bhāvasya nirodho nopapadyate |
nāsthitasyāpi bhāvasya nirodha upapadyate || 27

tayaivāvasthayāvasthā na hi saiva nirudhyate |
anyayāvasthayāvasthā na cānyaiva nirudhyate || 28

yadaivaṃ sarvadharmāṇām utpādo nopapadyate |
tadaivaṃ sarvadharmāṇāṃ nirodho nopapadyate || 29

sataś ca tāvad bhāvasya nirodho nopapadyate |
ekatve na hi bhavaś ca nābhāvaś copapadyate || 30

asato 'pi na bhāvasya nirodha upapadyate |
na dvitīyasya śirasaś chedanaṃ vidyate yathā || 31

na svātmanā nirodho 'sti nirodho na parātmanā |
utpādasya yathotpādo nātmanā na parātmanā || 32

utpādasthitibhaṅgānām asiddher nāsti samskrtam |
saṃskṛtasyāprasiddhau ca kathaṃ setsyaty asaṃskṛtam || 33

yathā māyā yathā svapno gandharvanagaraṃ yathā |
tathotpādas tathā sthānaṃ tathā bhaṅga udāhṛtam || 34

VIII

KARMA-KĀRAKA-PARĪKṢĀ

sadbhūtaḥ kārakaḥ karma sadbhūtaṃ na karoty ayam |
kārako nāpy asadbhūtaḥ karmāsadbhūtam īhate || 1

sadbhūtasya kriyā nāsti karma ca syād akaṛtvkam |
sadbhūtasya kriyā nāsti kartā ca syād akarmakaḥ || 2

karoti yady asadbhūto 'sadbhūtaṃ karma kārakaḥ |
ahetukaṃ bhavet karma kartā cāhetuko bhavet || 3

hetāv asati kāryaṃ ca kāraṇaṃ ca na vidyate |
tadabhāve kriyā kartā kāraṇaṃ ca na vidyate || 4

dharmādharmau na vidyete kriyādīnām asaṃbhave |
dharme cāsaty adharme ca phalaṃ tajjaṃ na vidyate || 5

phale 'sati na mokṣāya na svargāyopapadyate |
mārgaḥ sarvakriyāṇāṃ ca nairarthakyaṃ prasajyate || 6

kārakaḥ sadasadbhūtaḥ sadasat kurute na tat |
parasparaviruddhṃ hi sac cāsac caikataḥ kutaḥ || 7

satā ca kriyate nāsan nāsatā kriyate ca sat |
kartrā sarve prasajyānte doṣās tatra ta eva hi || 8

nāsadbhūtaṃ na sadbhūtaḥ sadasadbhūtam eva vā |
karoti kārakaḥ karma pūrvoktair eva hetubhiḥ || 9

nāsadbhūto 'pi sadbhūtaṃ sadasadbhūtam eva vā |
karoti kārakaḥ karma pūrvoktair eva hetubhiḥ || 10

karoti sadasadbhhūto na san nāsac ca kārakaḥ |
karma tat tu vijānīyāt pūrvoktair eva hetubhiḥ || 11

pratītya kārakaḥ karma taṃ pratītya ca kārakam |
karma pravartate nānyat paśyāmaḥ siddhikāraṇam || 12

evem vidyād upādānaṃ vyutsargād iti karmaṇaḥ |
kartuś ca karmakartṛbhyāṃ śeṣān bhāvān vibhāvayet || 13

IX

PŪRVA-PARĪKṢĀ

darśanaśravaṇādīni vedanādīni cāpy atha |
bhavanti yasya prāg ebhyaḥ so 'stīty eke vadantyuta || 1

kathaṃ hy avidyamānasya darśanādi bhaviṣyati |
bhāvasya tasmāt prāg ebhyaḥ so 'sti bhāvo vyavasthitaḥ || 2

darśanaśravaṇādibhyo vedanādibhya eva ca |
yaḥ prāg vyavasthito bhāvaḥ kena prajñapyate 'tha saḥ || 3

vināpi darśanādīni yadi cāsau vyavasthitaḥ |
amūny api bhaviṣyanti vinā tena na saṃśayaḥ || 4

ajyate kenacit kaścit kiṃcit kena cid ajyate |
kutaḥ kiṃcid vinā kaścit kiṃcit kaṃcid vinā kutaḥ || 5

sarvebhyo darśanādibhyaḥ kaścit pūrvo na vidyate |
ajyate darśanādīnām anyena punar anyadā || 6

sarvebhyo darśanādibhyo yadi pūrvo na vidyate |
ekaikasmāt kathaṃ pūrvo darśanādeḥ sa vidyate || 7

draṣṭā sa eva sa śrotā sa eva yadi vedakaḥ |
ekaikasmād bhavet pūrvam evaṃ caitan na yujyate || 8

draṣṭānya eva śrotānyo vedako 'nyaḥ punar yadi ||
sati syād draṣṭari śrotā bahutvaṃ cātmanāṃ bhavet || 9

darśanaśravaṇādīni vedanādīni cāpy atha |
bhavanti yebhyas teṣv eṣa bhūteṣv api na vidyate || 10

darśanaśravaṇādīni vedanādīni cāpy atha |
na vidyate ced yasya sa na vidyanta imāny api || 11

prāk ca yo darśanādibhyaḥ sāṃprataṃ cordhvam eva ca |
na vidyate 'sti nāstīti nivṛttās tatra kalpanāḥ || 12

X

AGNĪNDHANA-PARĪKṢĀ

yad indhanaṃ sa ced agnir ekatvaṃ kartṛkarmaṇoḥ |
anyaś ced indhanād agnir indhanād apy ṛte bhavet || 1

nityapradīpta eva syād apradīpanahetukaḥ |
punarārambhavaiyarthyam evaṃ cākarmakaḥ sati || 2

paratra nirapekṣatvād apradīpanahetukaḥ |
punarārambhavaiyarthyaṃ nityadīptaḥ prasajyate || 3

tatraitatsmād idhyamānam indhanam bhavatīti cet |
kenedhyatām indhanam tat tāvanmātram idaṃ yadā || 4

anyo na prāpsyate 'prapto na dhakṣyaty adahan punaḥ |
na nirvāsyaty anirvāṇaḥ sthāsyate vā svaliṅgavān || 5

anya evendhanād agnir indhanaṃ prāpnuyād yadi |
strī saṃprāpnoti puruṣaṃ puruṣaś ca striyaṃ yathā || 6

anya evendhanād agnir indhanaṃ kāmam āpnuyāt |
agnīndhane yadi syātām anyonyena tiraskṛte || 7

yadīndhanam apekṣyāgnir apekṣyāgniṃ yadīndhanam |
katarat pūrvaniṣpannaṃ yad apekṣyāgnir indhanam || 8

yadīndhanam apekṣyāgnir agneḥ siddhasya sādhanam |
evem satīndhanaṃ cāpi bhaviṣyati niragnikam || 9

yo 'pekṣya sidhyate bhāvas tam evāpekṣya sidhyati |
yadi yo 'pekṣitavyaḥ sa sidhyatāṃ kam apekṣya kaḥ || 10

yo 'pekṣya sidhyate bhāvaḥ so 'siddho 'pekṣate katham |
athāpy apekṣate siddhas tv apekṣāsya na yujyate || 11

apekṣyendhanam agnir na nānapekṣyāgnir indhanam |
apekṣyendhanam agniṃ na nānapekṣyāgnim indhanam || 12

āgacchaty anyato nāginir indhane 'gnir an vidyate |
atrendhane śeṣam uktaṃ gamyamānagatāgataiḥ || 13

indhanaṃ punar agnir na nāgnir anyatra cendhanāt |
nāgnir indhanavān nāgnāv indhanāni na teṣu saḥ || 14

agnīndhanābhyāṃ vyākhyāta ātmopādānayoḥ kramaḥ |
sarvo niravaśeṣeṇa sārdhaṃ ghaṭapaṭādibhiḥ || 15

ātmanaś ca satattvaṃ ye bhāvānāṃ ca pṛthak pṛthak |
nirdiśanti na tān manye śāsanasyārthakovidān || 16

XI

PŪRVĀPARA-KOṬI-PARĪKṢĀ

pūrvā prajñāyate koṭir nety uvāca mahāmuniḥ |
saṃsāro 'navarāgro hi nāsyādir nāpi paścimam || 1

naivāgraṃ nāvaraṃ yasya tasya madhyaṃ kuto bhavet |
tasmān nātropapadyante pūrvāparasahakramāḥ || 2

pūrvaṃ jātir yadi bhavej jarāmaraṇam uttaram |
nirjarāmaraṇā jātir bhavej jāyeta cāmṛtaḥ || 3

paścāj jātir yadi bhavej jarāmaraṇam āditaḥ |
ahetukam ajātasya syāj jarāmaraṇaṃ katham || 4

na jarāmaraṇenaiva jātiś ca saha yujyate |
mriyeta jāyamānaś ca syāc cāhetukatobhayoḥ || 5

yatra na prabhavanty ete pūrvāparasahakramāḥ |
prapañcayanti tāṃ jātiṃ taj jarāmaraṇaṃ ca kim || 6

kāryaṃ ca kāraṇaṃ caiva lakṣyaṃ lakṣaṇam eva ca |
vedanā vedakaś caivā santy arthā ye ca ke cana || 7

pūrvā na vidyate koṭiḥ saṃsārasya na kevalam |
sarveṣām api bhāvānāṃ pūrvā koṭir na vidyate || 8

XII

DUḤKHA-PARĪKṢĀ

svayaṃ kṛtaṃ parakṛtaṃ dvābhyāṃ kṛtam ahetukam |
duḥkham ity eka icchanti tac ca kāryaṃ na yujyate || 1

svayaṃ kṛtaṃ yadi bhavet pratītya na tato bhavet |
skandhān imān amī skandhāḥ saṃbhavanti pratītya hi || 2

yady amībhya ime 'nye syur ebhyo vāmī pare yadi |
bhavet parakṛtaṃ duḥkhaṃ parair ebhir amī kṛtāḥ || 3

svapudgalakṛtaṃ duḥkhaṃ yadi duḥkhaṃ punar vinā |
svapudgalaḥ sa katamo yena duḥkhaṃ svayaṃ kṛtam || 4

parapudgalajaṃ duḥkhaṃ yadi yasmai pradīyate |
pareṇa kṛtvā tad duḥkhaṃ sa duḥkhena vinā kutaḥ || 5

parapudgalajaṃ duḥkhaṃ yadi kaḥ parapudgalaḥ |
vina duḥkhena yaḥ kṛtvā parasmai prahiṇoti tat || 6

svayaṃ kṛtasyāprasiddher duḥkhaṃ parakṛtaṃ kutaḥ |
paro hi duḥkhaṃ yat kuryāt tat tasya syāt svayaṃ kṛtam || 7

na tāvat svakṛtaṃ duḥkhaṃ na hi tenaiva tat kṛtam |
paro nātmakṛtaś cet syād duḥkhaṃ parakṛtaṃ katham || 8

syād ubhābhyāṃ kṛtaṃ duḥkhaṃ syād ekaikakṛtaṃ yadi ||
parākārāsvayaṃkāraṃ duḥkham āhetukaṃ kutaḥ || 9

na kevalaṃ hi kuḥkhasya cāturvidhyaṃ na vidyate |
bāhyānām api bhāvānāṃ cāturvidhyaṃ na vidyate || 10

XIII

SAṂSKĀRA-PARĪKṢĀ

tan mṛṣā moṣadharma yad bhagavān ity abhāṣata |
sarve ca moṣadharmāṇaḥ saṃskārās tena te mṛṣā || 1

tan mṛṣā moṣadharma yad yadi kiṃ tatra muṣyate |
etat tūktaṃ bhagavatā śūnyatāparidīpakam || 2

bhāvānāṃ niḥsvabhāvatvam anyathābhāvadarśanāt |
nāsvabhāvaś ca bhāvo 'sti bhāvānāṃ śūnyatā yatah || 3

kasya syād anyathābhāvaḥ svabhāvaś cen na vidyate |
kasya syād anyathābhāvaḥ svabhāvo yadi vidyate || 4

tasyaiva nānyathābhāvo nāpy anyasyaiva yujyate |
yuvā na jīryate yasmād yasmāj jīrṇo na jīryate || 5

tasya ced anyāthābhavaḥ kṣīram eva bhaved dadhi |
ksīrād anyasya kasy ātha dadhibhāvo bhaviṣyati || 6

yady aśūnyaṃ bhavet kiṃcit syāc chūnyam api kiṃ cana |
na kiṃcid asty aśūnyaṃ ca kutaḥ śūnyaṃ bhaviṣyati || 7

śūnyatā sarvadṛṣṭīnāṃ proktā niḥsaraṇaṃ jinaiḥ |
yeṣāṃ tu śūnyatādṛṣṭis tān asādhyān babhāṣire || 8

XIV

SAṂSARGA-PARĪKṢĀ

draṣṭavyaṃ darśanaṃ draṣṭā trīṇy etāni dviśo dviśaḥ |
sarvaśaś ca na saṃsargam anyonyena vrajanty uta || 1

evaṃ rāgaś ca raktaś ca rañjanīyaṃ ca dṛśyatām |
traidhena śeṣāḥ kleśāś ca śeṣāṇy āyatanāni ca || 2

anyenānyasya saṃsargas tac cānyatvaṃ na vidyate |
draṣṭavyaprabhṛtīnāṃ yan na saṃsargaṃ vrajanty ataḥ || 3

na ca kevalam anyatvaṃ draṣṭavyāder na vidyate |
kasyacit kenacit sārdhaṃ nānyatvam upapadyate || 4

anyad anyat pratītyānyan nānyad anyad ṛte 'nyataḥ |
yat pratītya ca yat tasmāt tad anyan nopapadyate || 5

yady anyad anyad anyasmād anyasmād apy ṛte bhavet |
tad anyad anyad anyasmād ṛte nāsti ca nāsty ataḥ || 6

nānyasmin vidyate 'nyatvam ananyasmin na vidyate |
avidyamāne cānyatve nāsty anyad vā tad eva vā || 7

na tena tasqya saṃsargo nānyenānyasya yujyate |
saṃsṛjyamānaṃ saṃsṛṣṭaṃ saṃsraṣṭā ca na vidyate || 8

XV

SVABHĀVA-PARĪKṢĀ

na saṃbhavaḥ svabhāvasya yuktaḥ pratyayahetubhiḥ |
hetupratyayasaṃbhūtaḥ svabhāvaḥ kṛtako bhavet || 1

svabhāvaḥ kṛtako nāma bhaviṣyati punaḥ katham |
akṛtrimaḥ svabhāvo hi nirapekṣaḥ paratra ca || 2

kutaḥ svabhāvasyābhāve parabhāvo bhaviṣyati |
svabhāvaḥ parabhāvasya parabhāvo hi kathyate || 3

svabhāvaparabhāvābhyām ṛte bhāvaḥ kutaḥ punaḥ |
svabhāve parabhāve ca sati bhāvo hi sidhyati || 4

bhāvasya ced aprasiddhir abhāvo naiva sidhyati |
bhāvasya hy anyathābhāvam abhāvaṃ bruvate janāḥ || 5

svabhāvaṃ parabhāvaṃ ca bhāvaṃ cābhāvam eva ca |
ye paśyanti na paśyanti te tattvaṃ buddhaśāsane || 6

kātyāyanāvavāde cāstīti nāstīti cobhayam |
pratiṣiddhaṃ bhagavatā bhāvābhāvavibhāvinā || 7

yadi astitvaṃ prakṛtyā syān na bhaved asya nāstitā |
prakṛter anyathābhāvo na hi jātūpapadyate || 8

prakṛtau kasya cāsatyām anyathātvaṃ bhaviṣyati |
prakṛtau kasya cāsatyām anyathātvaṃ bhaviṣyati || 9

astīti śāśvatagrāho nāstity ucchedadarśanam |
tasmād astitvanāstitve nāśrīyeta vicakṣaṇaḥ || 10

asti yad dhi svabhāvena na tan nāstīti śāśvatam |
nāstīdānīm abhūt pūrvam ity ucchedaḥ prasajyate || 11

XVI

BANDHA-MOKṢA-PARĪKṢĀ

saṃskārāḥ saṃsaranti cen na nityāḥ saṃsaranti te |
saṃsaranti ca nānityāḥ sattve 'py eṣa samaḥ kramaḥ || 1

pudgalaḥ saṃsarati cet skandhāyatanadhātuṣu |
pañcadhā mṛgyamāṇo 'sau nāsti kaḥ saṃsariṣyati || 2

upādānād upādānaṃ saṃsaran vibhavo bhavet |
vibhavaś cānupādānaḥ kaḥ sa kiṃ saṃsariṣyati || 3

saṃskārāṇāṃ na nirvāṇaṃ kathaṃ cid upapadyate |
sattvasyāpi na nirvāṇaṃ kathaṃ cid upapadyate || 4

na badhyante na mucyanta udayavyayadharmiṇaḥ |
saṃskārāḥ pūrvavat sattvo badhyate na na mucyate || 5

bandhanaṃ ced upādānaṃ sopādāno na badhyate |
badhyate nānupādānaḥ kimavastho 'tha badhyate || 6

badhnīyād bandhanaṃ kāmaṃ bandhyāt pūrvaṃ bhaved yadi |
na casti tac cheṣam uktaṃ gamyamānagatāgataiḥ || 7

baddho na mucyate tāvad abaddho naiva mucyate |
syātāṃ baddhe mucyamāne yugapad bandhamokṣaṇe || 8

nirvāsyāmy anupādāno nirvāṇaṃ me bhaviṣyati |
iti yeṣāṃ grahas teṣām upādānamahāgrahaḥ || 9

na nirvāṇasamāropo na saṃsārāpakarṣaṇam |
yatra kas tatra saṃsāro nirvāṇaṃ kiṃ vikalpyate || 10

XVII

KARMA-PHALA PARĪKṢĀ

ātmasaṃyamakaṃ cetaḥ parānugrāhakaṃ ca yat |
maitraṃ sa dharmas tad bījaṃ phalasya pretya ceha ca || 1

cetanā cetayitvā ca karmoktaṃ paramarṣiṇā |
tasyānekavidho bhedaḥ karmaṇaḥ parikīrtitaḥ || 2

tatra yac cetanety uktaṃ karma tan mānasaṃ smṛtam |
cetayitvā ca yat tūktaṃ tat tu kāyikavācikam || 3

vāgviṣpando, viraṭāyo yāś cāvijñaptisaṃjñitāḥ |
avijñaptaya evānyāḥ smṛtā viratayas tathā || 4

paribhogānvayaṃ puṇyam apuṇyaṃ ca tathāvidham |
cetanā cety saptaite dharmāḥ karmāñjanāḥ smṛtāḥ || 5

tiṣṭhaty ā pākakālāc cet karma tan nityatām iyāt |
niruddhaṃ cen niruddhaṃ satkiṃ phalaṃ janayiṣyati || 6

yo 'nkuraprabhṛtir bījāt saṃtāno 'bhipravartate |
tataḥ phalam ṛte bījāt sa ca nābhipravartate || 7

bījāc ca yasmāt saṃtānaḥ saṃtānāc ca phalobhavaḥ |
bījapūrvaṃ phalāṃ tasmān nocchinnaṃ nāpi śāśvatam || 8

yas tasmāc cittasaṃtānaś cetaso 'bhipravartate |
tataḥ phalam ṛte cittāt sa ca nābhipravartate || 9

cittāc ca yasmāt saṃtānaḥ saṃtānāc ca phalodbhavaḥ |
karmapūrvaṃ phalaṃ tasmān nocchinnaṃ nāpi śāśvatam ||10

dharmasya sādhanopāyāḥ śuklāḥ karmapathā daśa |
phalaṃ kāmaguṇāḥ pañca dharmasya pretya ceha ca || 11

bahavaś ca mahāntaś ca doṣāḥ syur yadi kalpanā |
syād eṣā tena naivaiṣā kalpanātropapadyate || 12

imāṃ punaḥ pravakṣyāmi kalpanāṃ yātra yojyate |
buddhaiḥ pratyekabuddhaiś ca śrāvakaiś cānuvarṇitām || 13

pattraṃ yathā,vipraṇāśas tatharṇam iva karma ca |
caturvidho dhātutaḥ sa prakṛtyāvyākṛtaś ca saḥ || 14

prahāṇato na praheyo bhāvanāheya eva vā |
tasmād avipraṇāśena jāyate karmaṇāṃ phalam || 15

prhāṇataḥ praheyaḥ syāt karmaṇaḥ saṃkrameṇa vā |
yadi doṣāḥ prasajyeraṃs tatra karmavadhādayaḥ || 16

sarveṣāṃ visabhāgānāṃ sabhāgānāṃ ca karmaṇām |
pratiṣaṃdhau sadhātūnām eka utpadyate tu saḥ || 17

karmaṇaḥ karmaṇo dṛṣṭe dharma utpadyate tu saḥ |
dviprakārasya sarvasya vipakve 'pi ca tiṣṭhati || 18

phalavyatikramād vā sa maraṇād vā nirudhyate |
anāsravaṃ sāsravaṃ ca vibhāgaṃ tatra lakṣayet || 19

śūnyatā ca na cocchedaḥ saṃsāraś ca na śāśvatam |
karmaṇo 'vipranāśaś ca dharmo buddhena deśitaḥ || 20

karma notpadyate kasmān niḥsvabhāvaṃ yatas tataḥ |
yasmāc ca tad anutpannaṃ na tasmād vipraṇaśyati || 21

karma svabhāvataś cet syāc chāśvataṃ syād asaṃśayam |
akṛtaṃ ca bhavet karma kriyate na hi śāśvatam || 22

akṛtābhyāgamabhayaṃ syāt karmākṛtakaṃ yadi |
abrahmacaryavāsaś ca doṣas tatra prasajyate || 23

vyavahārā virudhyante sarva eva na saṃśayaḥ |
puṇyapāpakṛtor naiva pravibhāgaś ca yujyate || 24

tad vipakvavipākaṃ ca punar eva vipakṣyati |
karma vyavasthitaṃ yasmāt tasmāt svābhāvikaṃ yadi || 25

karma kleśātmakaṃ cedaṃ te ca kleśā na tattvataḥ |
na cet te tattvataḥ kleśāḥ karma syāt tattvataḥ katham || 26

karma kleśāś ca dehānāṁ pratyayāḥ samudāhṛtāḥ |
karma kleśāś ca te śūnyā yadi deheṣu kā kathā || 27

avidyānivṛto jantus tṛṣṇāsaṃyojanaś ca saḥ |
sa bhoktā sa ca na kartur anyo na ca sa eva saḥ || 28

na pratyayasamutpannaṃ nāpratyayasamutthitam |
asti yasmād idaṁ karma tasmāt kartāpi nāsty ataḥ || 29

karma cen nāsti kartā ca kutaḥ syāt karmajaṁ phalam |
asaty atha phale bhoktā kuta eva bhaviṣyati || 30

yathā nirmitakaṃ śāstā nirmimīta ṛddhisampadā |
nirmito nirmimītānyaṃ sa ca nirmitakaḥ punaḥ || 31

tathā nirmitakākāraḥ kartā yat karma tat kṛtam |
tadyathā nirmitenānyo nirmito nirmitas tathā || 32

kleśāḥ karmāṇi dehāś ca kartāraś ca phalāni ca |
gandharvanagarākāra marīcisvapnasaṁnibhāḥ || 33

XVIII

ĀTMA-PARĪKṢĀ

ātmā skandhā yadi bhaved udayavyayabhāg bhavet |
skandhedhyo 'nyo yadi bhaved bhaved askandha lakṣaṇaḥ || 1

ātmany asati cātmīyaṁ kuta eva bhaviṣyati |
nirmamo nirahaṃkāraḥ śamād ātmātmanīnayoḥ || 2

nirmamo nirahaṃkāro yaś ca so 'pi na vidyate |
nirmamaṃ nirahaṃkāraṃ yaḥ paśyati na paśyati || 3

mamety aham iti kṣīṇe bahirdhādhyātmam eva ca |
nirudhyata upādānaṃ tatṣayāj janmanaḥ kṣayaḥ || 4

karmakleśakṣayān mokṣaḥ karmakleśā vikalpataḥ |
te prapañcāt prapañcas tu śūnyatāyāṃ nirudhyate || 5

ātmety api prajñapitam anātmety api deśitam |
buddhair nātmā na cānātmā kaścid ity api deśitam || 6

nivṛttam abhidhātavyaṃ nivṛttaś cittagocaraḥ |
anutpannāniruddhā hi nirvāṇam iva dharmatā || 7

sarvam tathyaṃ na vā tathyaṃ tathyaṁ cātathyam eva ca |
naivātathyaṃ naiva tathyaṁ etad buddhānuśāsanam || 8

aparapratyayaṃ śāntaṁ prapañcair aprapañcitam |
nirvikalpam anānārtham etat tattvasya lakṣaṇam || 9

pratītya yad yad bhavati na hi tāvat tad eva tat |
nacānyad api tat tasmānnocchinnaṃnāpiśāśvatam || 10

anekārtham anānārtham anucchedam aśāśvatam |
etat tal lokanāthānāṃ buddhānāṃ śāsanāmṛtam || 11

sambuddhānām anutpāde śrāvakāṇāṃ punaḥ kṣaye |
jñānaṃ pratyekabuddhānāṁ asaṃsargāt pravartate || 12

XIX

KĀLA-PARĪKṢĀ

pratyutpanno 'nāgataś ca yady atītam apekṣka hi |
pratyutpanno 'nāgataś ca kāle 'tīte bhaviṣyataḥ || 1

pratyutpanno 'nāgataś ca na stas tatra punar yadi |
pratyutpanno 'nāgataś ca syātāṃ katham apekṣya tam || 2

anapekṣya punaḥ siddhir nātītaṁ vidyate tayoḥ |
pratyutpanno 'nāgataś ca tasmāt kālo na vidyate || 3

etenaivāvaśiṣṭau dvau kramena parivartakau |
uttamādhamamadhyādīn ekatvādīṃś ca lakṣayet || 4

nāsthito gṛhyate kālaḥ sthitaḥ kālo na vidyate |
yo gṛhyetāgṛhītaś ca kālaḥ prajñapyate katham || 5

bhāvaṃ pratītya kālaś cet kālo bhāvād ṛte kutaḥ |
na ca kaś cana bhāvo 'sti kutaḥ kālo bhaviṣyta || 6

XX

SĀMAGRI-PRĪKṢĀ

hetoś ca pratyayānāṃ ca sāmagryā jāyate yadi |
phalam asti ca sāmagryāṃ sāmagryā jāyate katham || 1

hetoś ca pratyayānāṃ ca sāmagryā jāyate yadi |
phalaṃ asti ca sāmagryāṃ sāmagryā jāyate katham || 2

hetoś ca pratyayānāṃ ca sāmagryām asti cet phalam |
gṛhyeta nanu sāmagryāṃ sāmagryāṃ ca na gṛhyate || 3

hetoś ca pratyayānāṃ ca sāmagryāṃ nāsti cet phalam |
hetavaḥ pratyayāś ca syur ahetupratyayaiḥ samāḥ || 4

hetuṃ phalasya dattvā ca yadi hetur nirudhyate |
yad dattaṃ yan niruddhaṃ ca hetor ātmadvayaṃ bhavet || 5

hetuṃ phalasyādattvā ca yadi hetur nirudhyate |
hetau niruddhe jātaṃ tat phalam āhetukaṃ bhavet || 6

phalaṃ sahaiva sāmagryā yadi prādurbhavet punaḥ |
ekakālau prasajyete janako yaś ca janyate || 7

pūrvam eva ca sāmagryāḥ phalaṃ prādurbhaved yadi |
hetupratyayanirmuktaṃ phalam āhetukaṃ bhavet || 8

niruddhe cet phalaṃ hetau hetoḥ saṃkramaṇaṃ bhavet |
pūrvajātasya hetoś ca punarjanma prasajyate || 9

janayet phalam utpannaṃ niruddho 'staṃgataḥ katham |
hetus tiṣṭhann api kathaṃ phalena janayed vṛtaḥ || 10

athāvṛtaḥ phalenāsau katamaj janayet phalam |
na hy adṛṣṭvā na dṛṣṭvāpi hetur janayate phalam || 11

nātītasya hy atītena phalasya saha hetunā |
nājātena na jātena saṃgatir jātu vidyate || 12

na jātasya hy ajātena phalasya saha hetunā |
nātītena na jātena saṃgatir jātu vidyate || 13

nājātasya hi jātena phalasya saha hetunā |
nājātena na naṣṭena saṃgatir jātu vidyate || 14

asatyāṃ saṃgatau hetuḥ kathaṃ janayate phalam |
satyāṃ vā saṃgatau hetuḥ kathaṃ janayate phalaṃ || 15

hetuḥ phalena śūnyaś cet kathaṃ janayate phalam |
hetuḥ phalenāśūnyaś cet kathaṃ janayate phalam || 16

phalaṃ notpatsyate 'śūnyam aśūnyaṃ na nirotsyate |
aniruddham anutpannam aśūnyaṃ tad bhaviṣyati || 17

katham utpatsyate śūnyaṃ kathaṃ śūnyaṃ nirotsyate |
śūnyam apy aniruddhaṃ tad anutpannaṃ prasajyate || 18

hetoḥ phalasya caikatvaṃ na hi jātūpapadyate |
hetoḥ phalsya cānyatvaṃ na hi jātūpapadyate || 19

ekatve phalahetvoḥ syād aikyaṃ janakajanyayoḥ |
pṛthaktve phalahetvoḥ syāt tulyo hetur ahetunā || 20

phalam svabhāvasadbhūtam kiṃ hetur janayiṣyati |
phalaṁ svabhāvāsadbhūtaṃ kiṃ hetur janayiṣyati || 21

na cājanayamānasya hetutvam upapadyate |
hetutvānupapattau ca phalaṃ kasya bhaviṣyati || 22

na ca pratyayahetūnām iyam ātmānam ātmanā |
yā sāmagrī janayate sā kathaṃ janayet phalam || 23

na sāmagrīkṛtaṃ phalaṃ nāsāmagrīkṛtaṃ phalam|
asti pratyayasāmagrī kuta eva phalaṁ vina || 24

XXI

SAṂBHAVA-VIBHAVA-PARĪKṢĀ

vinā vā saha va nāsti vibhavḥ saṁbhavena 'vai ।
vinā vā saha va nasti saṁbhavo vibhavena vai //

bhaviṣyati kathaṁ nāma vibhavaḥ saṁbhavaṃ vinā |
vinaiva janma maraṇaṃ vibhavo nodbhavaṃ vina || 2

saṃbhavenaiva vibhavaḥ kathaṃ saha bhaviṣyati |
na janma maraṇaṃ caivaṃ tulyakālaṃ hi vidyate || 3

bhaviṣyati kathaṃ nāma saṃbhavo vibhavaṃ vina |
anityatā hi bhaveṣu na kadācin na vidyate || 4

saṃbhavo vibhavenaiva kathaṃ saha bhaviṣyati |
na janma maraṇaṃ caiva tulyakālaṃ hi vidyate || 5

sahānyonyena vā siddhir vinānyonyena vā yayoḥ |
no vidyate tayoḥ siddhiḥ kathaṃ nu khalu vidyate || 6

kṣayasya saṃbhavo nāsti nākṣayasyāsti saṃbhavaḥ |
kṣayasya vibhavo nāsti vibhavo nākṣayasya ca || 7

saṃbhavo vibhavaś caiva vinā bhāvaṃ na vidyate |
saṃbhavaṃ vibhavaṃ caiva vina bhāvo na vidyate || 8

saṃbhavo vibhavaś caiva na śūnyasyopapadyate |
saṃbhavo vibhavaś caiva nāśūnyasyopapadyate || 9

saṃbhavo vibhavaś caiva naika ity upapadyate |
saṃbhavo vibhavaś caiva na nānety upapadyate || 10

dṛśyate saṃbhavaś caiva vibhavaś caiva te bhavet |
dṛśyate saṃbhavaś caiva mohād vibhava eva ca || 11

na bhāvāj jāyate bhāvo bhāvo 'bhāvān na jāyate |
nābhāvāj jāyate 'bhāvo 'bhāvo bhāvān na jāyate || 12

na svato jāyate bhāvaḥ parato naiva jāyate |
na svataḥ parataś caiva jāyate jāyate kutaḥ || 13

bhāvam abhyupapannasya śāśvatocchedadarśanam |
prasajyate sa bhāvo hi nityo 'nityo 'tha vā bhavet || 14

bhāvam abhyupapannasya naivocchedo na śāśvatam |
udayavyayasaṃtānaḥ phalahetvor bhavaḥ sa hi || 15

udayavyayasaṃtānaḥ phalahetvor bhavaḥ sa cet |
vyayasyāpunarutpatter hetūcchedaḥ prasajyate || 16

sadbhāvasya svabhāvena nāsadbhāvaś ca yujyate |
nirvāṇakāle cocchedaḥ praśamād bhavasaṃtateḥ || 17
carame na niruddhe ca prathamo yujyate bhavaḥ |
carame nāniruddhe ca prathamo yujyate bhavaḥ || 18
nirudhyamāne carame prathamo yadi jāyate |
nirudhyamāna ekaḥ syāj jāyamāno 'paro bhavet || 19

na cen nirudhyamānaś ca jāyamānaś ca yujyate |
sārdhaṃ ca mriyate yeṣu teṣu skandheṣu jāyate || 20

evaṃ triṣv api kāleṣu na yuktā bhavasaṃtatiḥ |
triṣu kāleṣu yā nāsti sā kathaṃ bhavasaṃtatiḥ || 21

XXII

TATHĀGATA-PARĪKṢĀ

skandhā na nānyaḥ skandhebhyo nāsmin skandhā na teṣu saḥ |
tathāgataḥ skandhavān na katamo 'tra tathāgataḥ || 1

buddhaḥ skandhān upādāya yadi nāsti svabhāvataḥ |
svabhāvataś ca yo nāsti kutaḥ sa parabhāvataḥ || 2

prtītya parabhāvaṃ yaḥ so 'nātmety upapadyate |
yaś cānātmā sa ca kathaṃ bhaviṣyati tathāgataḥ || 3

yadi nāsti svabhāvaś ca parabhāvaḥ kathaṃ bhavet |
svabhāvaparabhāvābhyām ṛte kaḥ sa tathāgataḥ || 4

skandhān yady anupādāya bhavet kaścit tathāgataḥ |
sa idānīm upādādyad upādāya tato bhavet || 5

skandhāṃś cāpy anupādāya nāsti kaścit tathāgataḥ |
yaś ca nāsti anupādāya sa upādāsyate katham || 6

na bhavaty anupādattam upādānaṃ ca kiṃ cana |
na-cāsti nirupādānaḥ kathaṃ cana tathāgataḥ || 7

tattvānyatvena yo nāsti mṛgyamāṇāś ca pañcadha |
upādānena sa kathaṃ prajñapyate tathāgataḥ || 8

yad apīdam upādānaṃ tat svabhāvān na vidyate |
svabhāvataś ca yan nāsti kutaś tat parabhāvataḥ || 9

evaṃ śūnyaṃ upādānam upādātā ca sarvaśaḥ |
prajñapyate ca śunyena kathaṃ śūnyas tathāgataḥ || 10

śūnyam iti na vaktavyam aśūnyam iti vā bhavet |
ubhayaṃ nobhayaṃ ceti prajñaptyarthaṃ tu kathyate || 11

śāśvatāśāśvatādy atra kutaḥ śānte catuṣṭayam |
antānantādi cāpy atra kutaḥ śānte catuṣṭayam || 12

ghanagrāho gṛhitas tu yenāstīti tathāgataḥ |
nāstīti sa vikalpayan nirvṛtasyāpi kalpayet || 13

svabhāvataś ca śūnye 'smiṃś cintā naivopapadyate |
paraṃ nirodhād bhavati buddho na bhavatīti vā || 14

prapañcayanti ye buddhaṃ prapañcātītam avyayam |
te prapañcahatāḥ sarve na paśyanti tathāgatam || 15

tathāgato yatsvabhāvas tatsvabhāvam idaṃ jagat |
tathāgato niḥsvabhāvo niḥsvabhāvam idaṃ jagat || 16

XXIII

VIPARYĀSA-PARĪKṢĀ

sāṃkalpaprabhavo rāgo dveṣo mohaś ca kathyate |
śubhāśubhaviparyāsān saṃbhavanti pratītya hi || 1

śubhāśubhaviparyāsān saṃbhavanti pratītya ye |
te svabhāvān na vidyante tasmāt kleśā na tattvataḥ || 2

ātmano 'stitvanāstitve na kathaṃ cic ca sidhyataḥ |
taṃ vināstitvanāstitve kleśānāṃ sidhyataḥ katham || 3

kasya cid dhi bhavantīme kleśāḥ sa ca na sidhyti |
kaścid āho vinā kaṃcit santi kleśā na kasyacit || 4

svakāyadṛṣṭivat kleśāḥ kliṣṭe santi na pañcadha |
svakāyadṛṣṭivat kliṣṭaṃ kleśeṣv api na pañcadhā || 5

svabhavato na vidyante śubhāśubhaviparyayāḥ |
pratītya katamān kleśāḥ śubhāśubhaviparyayān || 6

rūpaśabdarasasparśā gandhā dharmāś ca ṣaḍvidam |
vastu rāgasya doṣasya mohasya ca vikalpyate || 7

rūpaśabdarasasparśā gandha dharmāś ca kevalāḥ |
gandharvanagarākārā marīcisvapnasaṃnibhāḥ || 8

aśubhaṃ vā śubhaṃ vāpi kutas teṣu bhaviṣyati |
māyāpuruṣākalpeṣu pratibimbasameṣu ca || 9

anapekṣya śubhaṃ nāsty aśubhaṃ prajñapayemahi |
yat pratītya śubhaṃ tasmāc chubhaṃ naivopapadyate || 10

anapekṣyāśubhaṃ nāsti śubhaṃ prajñapayemahi |
yat pratītyāśubhaṃ tasmād aśubhaṃ naiva vidyate || 11

avidyamāne ca śubhe kuto rago bhaviṣyati |
aśubhe 'vidyamāne ca kuto dveṣo bhaviṣyati || 12

anitye nityam ity evaṃ yadi grāho viparyayaḥ |
nānityaṃ vidyate śūnye kuto grāho viparyayaḥ || 13

anitye nityam ity evaṃ yadi grāho viparyayaḥ |
anityam ity api grāhaḥ śūnye kiṃ na viparyayaḥ || 14

yena gṛhṇāti yo grāho grahītā yac ca gṛhyate |
upaśāntāni sarvāṇi tasmād grāho na vidyate || 15

avidyamāne grāhe ca mithyā vā samyag eva vā |
bhaved viparyayaḥ kasya bhavet kasyāviparyayaḥ || 16

na cāpi viparītasya saṃbhavanti viparyayāḥ |
na cāpy aviparītasya saṃbhavanti viaryayāḥ || 17

na viparyasyamānasya saṃbhavanti viparyayāḥ |
vimṛśasva svayaṃ kasya saṃbhavanti viparyayāḥ || 18

anutpannāḥ kathaṃ nāma bhaviṣyanti viparyayāḥ |
viparyayeṣv ajāteṣu viparyayagataḥ kutaḥ || 19

na svato jāyate bhāvaḥ parato naiva jāyate |
na svataḥ parataś ceti viparyayagataḥ kutaḥ || 20

ātmā ca śuci nityaṃ ca sukhaṃ ca yadi vidyate |
ātmā ca śuci nityaṃ ca sukhaṃ ca na viparyayaḥ || 21

nātmā ca 'śuci nityaṃ ca sukhaṃ ca yadi vidyate |
anātmā śucy anityaṃ ca naiva duḥkhaṃ ca vidyate || 22

evaṃ nirudhyate 'vidyā viparyayanirodhanāt |
avidyāyāṃ niruddhāyāṃ saṃskārādyaṃ nirudhyate || 23

yadi bhūtāḥ svabhāvena kleśāḥ kecid dhi kasyacit |
kathaṃ nāma prahīyeran kaḥ svabhāvaṃ prahāsyati || 24

yady abhūtāḥ svabhāvena kleśāḥ kecid dhi kasyacit |
kathaṃ nāma prahīyeran ko 'sadbhāvaṃ prahāsyati || 25

XXIV

ĀRYASATYA-PARĪKṢĀ

yadi śūnyam idaṃ sarvam udayo nāsti na vyayaḥ |
caturṇām āryasatyānām abhāvas te prasajyate || 1

parijñā ca prahāṇaṃ ca bhāvanā sākṣikarma ca |
caturṇām āryasatyānām abhāvān nopapadyate || 2

tadabhāvān na vidyante catvāry āryaphalāni ca |
phalābhāve phalasthā no na santi pratipannakāḥ || 3

saṃgho nāsti na cet santi te 'ṣṭau puruṣapudgalāḥ |
abhāvāc cāryastyānāṃ saddharmo 'pi na vidyate || 4

dharme cāsati saṃghe ca kathaṃ buddho bhaviṣyati |
evaṃ trīṇy api ratnāni bruvāṇaḥ pratibādhase || 5

śūnyatāṃ phalasadbhāvam adharmaṃ dharmam eva ca |
śarvasaṃvyavahārāṃś ca laukikān pratibādhase || 6

atra brūmaḥ śūnyatāyāṃ na tvaṃ vetsi prayojanam |
śūnyatāṃ śūnyatārthaṃ ca tata evaṃ vihanyase || 7

dve satye samupāśritya buddhānāṃ dharmadeśanā |
lokasaṃvṛtisatyaṃ ca satyaṃ ca paramārthataḥ || 8

ye 'nayor na vijānanti vibhāgaṃ satyayor dvayoḥ |
te tattvaṃ na vijānanti gambhīraṃ buddhaśāsane || 9

vyavahāram anāśritya paramārtho na deśyate |
paramārtham anāgamya nirvāṇaṃ nādhigamyate || 10

vināśayati durdṛṣṭā śūnyatā mandamedhasam |
sarpo yathā durgṛhīto vidyā vā duṣprasādhitā || 11

ataś ca pratyudāvṛttaṃ cittaṃ deśayituṃ muneḥ |
dharmaṃ matvāsya dharmasya mandair duravagāhatām || 12

śūnyatāyām adhilayaṃ yaṅ punaḥ kurute bhavān |
doṣaprasaṅgo nāsmākaṃ sa.śūnye nopapadyate | 13

sarvaṃ ca yujyate tasya śūnyatā yasya yujyate |
sarvaṃ na yujyate tasya śūyaṃ yasya na yujyate || 14

sa tvaṃ doṣān ātmanīyān asmāsu paripātayan |
aśvam evābhirūḍhaḥ sann aśvam evāsi vismṛtaḥ || 15

svabhāvād yadi bhāvānāṃ sadbhāvam anupaśyasi |
ahetupratyayān bhāvāṃs tvam evaṃ sati paśyasi || 16

kāryaṃ ca kāraṇam caiva kartāraṃ karaṇam kriyām |
utpādaṃ ca nirodhaṃ ca phalaṃ ca pratibādhase || 17

yaḥ pratītyasamutpādaḥ śūyatāṃ tāṃ pracakṣmahe |
sā prajñaptir upādāya pratipat saiva madhyamā || 18

apratītya samutpanno dharmaḥ kaścin na vidyate |
yasmāt tasmād aśūnyo hi dharmaḥ kaścin na vidyate || 19

yady aśūnyam idaṃ sarvam udayo nāsti na vyayaḥ |
caturṇām āryasatyānām abhāvas te prasajyate || 20

apratītya samutpannaṃ kuto duḥkhaṃ bhaviṣyati |
anityam uktaṃ duḥdhaṃ hi tat svābhāvye na vidyate || 21

svabhāvato vidyamānaṃ kiṃ punaḥ samudeśyate |
tasmāt samudayo nāsti śūnyatāṃ pratibādhataḥ || 22

na nirodhaḥ svabhāvena sato duḥkhasya vidyate |
svabhāvaparyavasthānān nirodhaṃ pratibādhase || 23

svābhāvye sati mārgasya bhāvanā nopapadyate |
athāsau bhāvyate mārgaḥ svābhāvyaṃ tena vidyate || 24

yadā duḥkhaṃ samudayo nirodhaś ca na vidyate |
mārgo duḥkhanirodhatvāt katamaḥ prāpayiṣyati || 25

svabhāvenāparijñānaṃ yadi tasya punaḥ katham |
parijñānaṃ nánu kila svabhāvaḥ samavasthitaḥ || 26

prahāṇasākṣātkaraṇe bhāvanā caivam eva te |
parijñāvan na yujyate catvāry api phalāni ca || 27

svabhāvenānadhigataṃ yat phalaṃ tat punaḥ katham |
śakyaṃ samadhigantuṃ syāt svabhāvaṃ parigṛhṇataḥ || 28

phalābhāve phalastha no na santi pratipannakāḥ |
saṃgho nāsti na cet santi te 'ṣṭau puruṣapudgalāḥ || 29

abhāvāc cāryasatyānāṃ saddharmo 'pi na vidyate m |
dharme cāsati saṃghe ca kathaṃ buddho bhaviṣyati || 30

apratītyāpi bodhiṃ ca tava buddhaḥ prasajyate |
apratītyāpi buddhaṃ ca tava bodhiḥ prasajyate || 31

yaś cābuddhaḥ svabhāvena sā bodhāya ghaṭann api |
na bodhisattvacaryāyāṃ bodhiṃ to 'dhigamiṣyati || 32

na ca dharmam adharmaṃ vā kaścij jātu kariṣyati |
kim aśūnyasya kartavyaṃ svabhāvaḥ kriyate na hi || 33

vinā dharmam adharmaṃ ca phalaṃ hi tava vidyate |
dharmādharmanimittaṃ ca phalaṃ tava na vidyate || 34

dharmādharmanimittaṃ vā yadi te vidyate phalam /
dharmādharmasamutpannam aśūnyaṃ te kathaṃ phalam // 35

sarvasaṃvyavahārāṃs ca laukikān pratibādhase /
yat pratītyasamutpādaśūnyatām pratibādhase // 36

na kartavyaṃ bhavet kiṃcid anārabdhā bhavet kriyā /
kārakaḥ syād akurvāṇaḥ śūnyatāṃ pratibādhataḥ // 37

ajātam aniruddhaṃ ca kūṭasthaṃ ca bhaviṣyati /
vicitrābhir avasthābhiḥ svabhāve rahitaṃ jagat // 38

asamprāptasya ca prāptir duḥkhaparyantakarma ca /
sarvakleśaprahāṇaṃ ca yady aśūnyaṃ na vidyate // 39

yaḥ pratītyasamutpādaṃ paśyatīdaṃ sa paśyati /
duḥkhaṃ samudayaṃ caiva nirodhaṃ mārgam eva ca // 40

XXV

NIRVĀṆA - PARĪKṢĀ

yadi śūnyam idaṃ sarvam udayo nāsti na vyayaḥ |
prahāṇād vā nirodhād vā kasya nirvāṇam iṣyate || 1

yady aśūnyam idaṃ sarvam udayo nāsti na vyayaḥ |
prahāṇād vā nirodhād vā kasya nirvāṇam iṣyate || 2

aprahīṇam asaṃprāptam anucchinnam aśāśvatam |
aniruddham anutpannam etan nirvāṇam ucyate || 3

bhāvas tāvan na nirvāṇaṃ jarāmaraṇalakṣaṇam |
prasajyetāsti bhāvo hi na jarāmaraṇaṃ vinā || 4

bhāvaś ca yadi nirvāṇam nirvāṇaṃ saṃskṛtaṃ bhavet |
nāsaṃskṛto hi vidyate bhāvaḥ kva cana kaś cana || 5

bhāvaś ca yadi nirvāṇam anupādāya tat katham |
nirvāṇaṃ nānupādāya kaścid bhāvo hi vidyate || 6

bhāvo yadi na nirvāṇam abhāvaḥ kiṃ bhaviṣyati |
nirvāṇaṃ yatra bhāvo na nābhāvas tatra vidyate || 7

yady abhāvaś ca nirvāṇam anupādāya tat katham |
nirvāṇaṃ na hy abhāvo 'sti yo 'nupādāya vidyate || 8

ya ājavaṃjavībhāva upādāya pratītya vā |
so 'pratītyānupādāya nirvāṇam upadiśyate || 9

prahāṇaṃ cābravīc chāstā bhavasya vibhavasyas ca |
tasmān na bhāvo nābhāvo nirvāṇam iti yujyate || 10

bhaved abhāvo bhāvaś ca nirvāṇam ubhayaṃ yadi |
bhaved abhāvo bhāvaś ca mokṣas tac ca na yujyate || 11

bhaved abhāvo bhāvaś ca nirvāṇam ubhayaṃ yadi |
nānupādāya nirvāṇam upādāyobhayaṃ hi tat || 12

bhaved abhāvo bhāvaś ca nirvāṇam ubhayaṃ katham |
asaṃskṛtaṃ hi nirvāṇaṃ bhāvābhāvaucasaṃskṛtau || 13

bhaved abhāvo bhāvaś ca nirvāṇa ubhayam katham |
tayor abhāvo hy ekatra prakāśatamasor iva || 14

naivābhāvo naiva bhāvo nirvāṇaṃ iti yā 'ñjanā |
abhāve caiva bhāve ca sā siddhe sati sidhyati || 15

naivābhāvo naiva bhāvo nirvāṇaṃ yadi vidyate |
naivābhāvo naiva bhāva iti kena tad ajyate || 16

paraṃ nirodhād bhagavān bhavatīty eva nājyate |
na bhavaty ubhayaṃ ceti nobhayaṃ ceti nājyate || 17

tiṣṭhamāno 'pi bhagavān bhavatīty eva nājyate |
na bhavaty ubhayaṃceti nobhayaṃ ceti nājyate || 18

na saṃsārasya nirvāṇāt kiṃcid asti viśeṣaṇam |
na nirvāṇasya saṃsārāt kiṃcid asti viśeṣaṇam || 19

nirvāṇasya ca yā koṭiḥ koṭiḥ saṃsaraṇasya ca |
na tayor antaraṃ kiṃcit susūkṣmam api vidyate || 20

paraṃ nirodhād antādyāḥ śāśvatādyāś ca dṛṣṭayaḥ |
nirvāṇam aparāntaṃ ca pūrvāntaṃ ca samāśritāḥ || 21

śūnyeṣu sarvadharmeṣu kim anantaṃ kim antavat ||
kim anantam antavac ca nānantaṃ nāntavac ca kim || 22

kiṃ tad eva kim anyat kiṃ śāśvataṃ kim aśāśvatam |
aśāśvataṃ śāśvataṃ ca kiṃ vā nobhayam apy atha || 23

sarvopalambhopaśamaḥ prapañcopaśamaḥ śivaḥ |
na kva cit kas'yacit kas'cid dharmo buddhena desitah || 24

XXVI

DVĀDAŚĀṄGA-PARĪKṢĀ

punarbhavāya saṃskārān avidyānivṛtas tridhā |
abhisaṃskurute yāṃs tair gatiṃ gacchati karmabhiḥ || 1

vijñānaṃ samniviśate saṃskārapratyayaṃ gatau |
samniviṣṭe 'tha vijñāne nāmarūpaṃ niṣicyate || 2

niṣikte nāmarūpe tu ṣaḍāyatanasaṃbhavaḥ |
sadayatanam āgamya saṃsparśaḥ sampravartate || 3

caksuḥ pratītya rūpaṃ ca samanvāhāram eva ca |
nāmarupam pratītyaivam vijñānaṃ saṃpravartate || 4
samnipātas trayāṇāṃ yo rūpa vijñānacakṣuṣam ||
spars'ahsa tasmāt sparśāc ca vedanā saṃpravartate || 5

vedanāpratyayā tṛṣṇā vedanārthaṃ hi tṛṣyate |
tṛṣyamāṇa upādānam upādatte caturvidham || 6

upādāne sati bhava upādātuḥ pravartate |
syād dhi yady anupādāno mucyeta na bhaved bhavaḥ || 7

pañca skandhāḥ sa ca bhavo bhavāj jātiḥ pravartate |
jarāmaraṇaduḥkhādi śokāḥ saparidevanāḥ || 8

daurmanasyam upāyāsā jāter etat pravartate |
kevalasyaivam etasya duḥkhaskandhasya saṃbhavaḥ || 9

saṃsāramūlaṃ saṃskārān avidvān saṃskaroty ataḥ |
avidvān kārakas tasmān na vidvāṃs tattvadarśanāt || 10

avidyāyāṃ niruddhāyāṃ saṃskārāṇām asaṃbhavaḥ |
avidyāyā nirodhas tu jñānasyāsyaiva bhāvanāt || 11

tasya tasya nirodhena tat tan nābhipravartate |
duḥkhaskandhaḥ kevalo 'yam evaṃ samyag nirudhyate || 12

XXVII

DṚṢṬI-PARĪKṢĀ

abhūm atītam adhvānaṃ nābhūvam iti dṛṣṭayaḥ |
yās tāḥ śāśvatalokādyāḥ pūrvāntaṃ samupāśritāḥ || 1

dṛṣṭayo na bhaviṣyāmi kim anyo 'nāgate 'dhvani |
bhaviṣyāmīti cāntādyā aparāntaṃ samāśritāḥ || 2

abhūm atītam adhvānam ity etan nopapadyate |
yo hi janmasu pūrveṣu sa eva na bhavaty ayam || 3

sa evātmeti tu bhaved upādānaṃ viśiṣyate |
upādānavinirmukta ātmā te katamaḥ punaḥ || 4

upādānavinirmukto nāsty ātmeti kṛte sati |
syād upādānam evātmā nāsti cātmeti vaḥ punaḥ || 5

na copādānam evātmā vyeti tat samudeti ca |
kathaṃ hi nāmopādānam upādātā bhaviṣyati || 6

anyaḥ punar upādānād ātmā naivopapadyate |
gṛhyeta hy anupādāno yady anyo na ca gṛhyate || 7

evaṃ nānya upādānān na copādānam eva saḥ |
ātmā nāsty anupādāno nāpi nāsty eṣa niścayaḥ || 8

nābhum atītam adhvānam ity etan nopapadyate |
yo hi janmasu pūrveṣu tato 'nyo na bhavaty ayam || 9

yadi hy ayaṃ bhaved anyaḥ pratyākhyāyāpitaṃ bhavet |
tathaiva ca sa saṃtiṣṭhet tatra jāyeta cāmṛtaḥ || 10

ucchedaḥ karmaṇāṃ nāśaḥ kṛtam anyena karma ca |
pratisaṃvedayed anya evam ādi prasajyate || 11

nāpy abhūtvā samudbhūto doṣo hy atra prasajyate |
kṛtako vā bhaved ātmā saṃbhūto vāpy ahetukaḥ || 12

evaṃ dṛṣṭir atīte yā nābhūm aham abhūm aham |
ubhayaṃ nobhayaṃ ceti naiṣā samupapadyate || 13

adhvany anāgate kiṃ nu bhaviṣyāmīti darśanam |
na bhaviṣyāmi cety etad atītenādhvanā samam || 14

sa devaḥ sa manuṣyaś ced evaṃ bhavati śāśvatam |
anutpannaś ca devaḥ syāj jāyate na hi śāśvatam | 15

devād anyo manuṣyaś ced aśāśvatam ato bhavet |
devād anyo manuṣyaś cet saṃtatir nopapadyate || 16

divyo yady ekadeśaḥ syād ekadeśaś ca mānuṣaḥ |
aśāśvataṃ śāśvataṃ ca bhavet tac ca na yujyate || 17

aśāśvataṃ śāśvataṃ ca prasiddham ubhayaṃ yadi |
siddhe na śāśvataṃ kāmaṃ naivāśāśvatam ity api || 18

kutaścid āgataḥ kaścit kiṃcid gacchet punaḥ kva cit |
yadi tasmād anādis tu saṃsāraḥ syān na cāsti saḥ || 19

nāsti cec chāśvataḥ kaścit ko bhaviṣyaty aśāśvataḥ |
śāśvato' śāśvataś cāpi dvābhyām ābhyāṃ tiraskṛtaḥ || 20

antavān yadi lokaḥ syāt paralokaḥ kathaṃ bhavet |
athāpy anantavāl lokaḥ paralokaḥ kathaṃ bhavet || 21

skandhānām eṣa saṃtāno yasmād dīpārciṣām iva |
tasmān nānantavattvaṃ ca nāntavattvaṃ ca yujyate || 22

pūrve yadi ca bhajyerann utpadyeran na cāpy amī |
skandhāḥ skandhān pratītyemān atha loko 'ntavān bhavet ||23

pūrve yadi na bhajyerann utpadyeran na cāpy amī |
skandhāḥ skandhān pratītyemāl loko'nanto bhaved atha || 24

antavān ekadeśaś ced ekadeśas tv anantavān |
syād antavān anantaś ca lokas tac ca na yujyate || 25

kathaṃ tāvad upādātur ekadeśo vinaṅkṣyate |
na naṅkṣyate caikadeśa evaṃ caitan na yujyate || 26

upādānaikadeśaś ca kathaṃ nāma vinaṅkṣyate |
na naṅkṣyate caikadeśo naitad apy upapadyate || 27

antavac cāpy anantaṃ ca prasiddham ubhayaṃ yadi |
siddhe naivāntavat kāmaṃ naivānantavad ity api || 28

atha vā sarvabhāvānāṃ śūnyatvāc chāśvatādayaḥ |
kva kasya katamāḥ kasmāt saṃbhaviṣyanti dṛṣṭayaḥ || 29

sarvadṛṣṭiprahāṇāya yaḥ saddharmam adeśayat |
anukampāmupādāya taṃ namasyāmi gautamam || 30

KĀRIKĀ INDEX

PART III

Supplementary Reading

- Seventy Stanzas on śūnyatā (Śūnyatā-Saptati)
- A Treatise on the Rejection of Contentions
- Vigraha-vyāvartani-kārikāḥ
- Index of Kārikās

NĀGĀRJUNA'S

(Sūnyatā - Saptati : Tibetan Version)

SEVENTY STANZAS ON ŚŪNYATĀ

1. The Buddha talked of endurance; origination, destruction, existence; non -existence, low, middle, high in keeping with worldly transactions; but not because these are dictacted by truth.

2. Language is nothing, as soul, no-soul, and soul-no-soul do not exist. Things we talk about being devoid of identity are *Nirvāṇa-like.*

3. All things in every respect being deviod of identity, do not exist in causes or relativity or in their totality or in isolation. Thus, they are *s'ūnya.*

4. Existence would not originate because it would have to come to exist. Non-existence would not originate as it would not exist. Existence-non-existence would not arise, because it would be contradictory. Therefore, they would have no endurance and destruction.

5. That which is already born cannot be born; that which is yet to be born cannot be born. That which is being born being partly unborn cannot be born.

6. A cause has to have an effect present. The effect already produced in the past and the effect not yet produced would render a cause as no-cause, as they have no existence. The effect being born, being both existent and non-existent, would be contradictory. Thus it is not justified to get a cause in all the three time.

7. Without 'one', there cannot be 'many' and without there being 'many' 'one' would not be possible. Therefore, things produced relatively would lack the basis for their determination.

8. Suffering having origination relative to twelve links is unborn, as it would not be possible to locate this suffering in one or many minds.

9. There is no eternality, no non-eternality; there is no soul, no non-soul; there is nothing pure, nothing not-pure; there is no pleasure, no suffering. Thus perversion is not possible.

10. In the absence of these, ignorance arising on account of perversion is not possible. As ignorance does not exist, impressions would not arise, so also the remaining links.

11. Ignorance having no impressions would not exist and likewise, without ignorance impressions would not arise. They being relative to each other have no identity.

12. How could a thing, not determined by its identity, create others? Therefore, relativity determined by others cannot create others.

13. There is no father without a son and there is no son without a father. Neither of them exists without mutual relativity. They cannot also be simultaneous. So are the twelve links.

14. Like pleasure and pain arising relative to objects appearing in a dream have no real object, similarly neither the object arising in relativity nor the one originating an object in relativity has existence.

15. (The opponent says that) If things exist without identity, multi-faceted world having low, middle and high points would not be established. No cause would establish them either.

16. (The Mādhyamika says that) If identity could be established things originating in relativity would not arise. If they have no existence in relativity, why should identity be lacking in them, as identity connot become non-existent.

17. How could a non-existing entity have identity of its own or from others or from non-existence? Therefore, identity of one's own, identity from others or identity from non-existence is perversion.

18. (Opponent may say that) If things are *s'ūnya,* origination and cessasion would not be possible. That which be *s'ūnya* in its identity, how could it cease or originate?

19. (The Mādhyamika says that) Existence and non-existence do not exist together. There is not existence in the absence of non-existence. Existence and non-existence are always there. Thus there is no existence not relative to non-existence.

20. Without existence there is no non-existence. It does not arise by itself or because of others. This being so, there is neither existence nor non-existence.

21. If there is existence, there is eternality; if there is non-existence, there is necessarily annihilation. These two defects take place on account of existence. Thus existence should not be accepted.

22. (The oponent may say that) This may not hold, because existence being a series, it would cease to be after causing the next moment. (The Mādhyamika replies that) The series itself is unestablished. Moreover, the series would be interrupted.

23. (The opponent, further, may say that) The teaching about the path by the Buddha shows that origination and cessation are not *s'ūnya*. (The Mādhyamika replies that) To think that the two are mutually excluding is a perversion.

24. (The opponent may say that) In the absense of origination and cessation, Nirvāṇa would be due to the cessation of what? (The Mādhyamika answers that) Is it not that liberation by nature is such that nothing arises and ceases to be there?

25. If Nirvāṇa were to arise from cessation, it would be nihilistic. If it were to be otherwise it would be eternal. Thus Nirvāṇa cannot be justified either as existent or as non-existent.

26. If cessation were to persist, Nirvāṇa would became without an existent. It would not be possible without an existent nor without a non-existent entity.

27. An identifying characteristic different from what is being identified would establish what is to be identified. It would neither be established by itself nor would the two establish each other. What is not established itself cannot establish anything unestablished.

28. Thus are explained cause, effect, feeling, he who has feeling, etc. and the one who sees and the object of seeing etc. and all other entities without exception.

29. The three times do not exist because they are not determined. They cannot determine each other, nor are they self-determined. Because they change, there is no existence. They are only mental constructions.

30. Since three characteristics of composite entities viz. origination, endurance and cessation do not exist, there is nothing like a composite or a non-composite entity.

31. That which is not destroyed does not cease, nor does that which is already destroyed. The enduring thing does not endure, nor does the non-enduring endure. A thing born does not originate, not does that originate which is not born.

32. Composite and non-composite entities are neither manifold nor unitary; they neither exist, nor do not exist, they are not existent-and-non-existent. Everything should be understood this way.

33. (The opponent says that) The great sage Lord Buddha spoke of endurance of action, the nature of action and the result of action. He also spoke of action done by living beings and its non-destruction.

34. (The Mādhyamika says that) Action has no identity. A non-originated action is not destroyed and gives rise to 'I-sense' (ahaṃkāra). Mental construction makes it hold fast.

35. If action were to have identity, the body created by it would become eternal; action done would not generate suffering and it would have been substantial.

36. Action does not originate either in relativity or in non-relativity. Impressions created by action are like magic, a city appearing in the sky and mirage.

37. Action is caused by afflictions. Impressions being afflictions are like action. A body being caused by action is devoid of identity.

38. There is no agent without action and in the absence of these two there is no result. Without these three no enjoyer is possible. Therefore things are distinct.

39. He who perceives truth correctly that action is *s'ūnya*, to him action does not originate and thus nothing further arises relative to action.

40-42. The Buddha may artificially create a being by his spiritual power and this artificially created being may in his turn create another artificial being. The being created by the Buddha is *s'ūnya*, so is the other artificially created being. They are just names posited by mental construction. Similar is the agent an aritifcially created being; his action is similar to the artificially created being by another being himself so created. They are devoid of identity and are posited by mental construction.

43. If action had identity, Nirvāṇa would not be possible nor would the action done by an agent. In the absence of action pleasure and suffering would not be possible.

44. The Buddha talked of 'is', 'is not', and also of 'both is and is not', with some intention which cannot be easily comprehended.

45. If form were material it could not arise out of material elements. It would not be self-created nor would it come into existence as created by others. Thus it does not exist.

46. Of the four elements, one form does not exist in all the four nor all of them do exist in one form. How would form be established having been created by four elements?

47. Because form is not directly apprehended, it therefore does not exist. If it were to be comprehended through a mark, that mark itself being created by causes and relativity would have no existence. Its existence without a mark cannot be justified

48. If form were to be comprehended by mind, it should comprehend its identity. But since mind exists in relativity, it would not comprehend a form.

49. As already explained, one moment of mind cannot comprehend within the same moment a form presently created. How could it comprehend a past or a future form.

50. Since colour and pattern never exist apart they would not be comprehended separately. But form is accepted to be unitary.

51. Seeing does not exist in the eyes; it does not exist in form seen, nor does it exist in both of them. The image arising relative to form and eyes is thus false.

52. If eye does not see itself, how can it see form? Therefore both the eyes and the form are non-substantial. So is the case with other bases of sense organs.

53. Eye is *s'ūnya* of own nature; it is also *s'ūnya* of other's nature. Similarly form is *s'ūnya* and so are other sense-organs.

54. One sense-organ cannot come in contact with an object as that is *s'ūnya*. *Śūnya* cannot be relative to non *s'ūnya* and *non-s'ūnya* cannot be relative to *s'ūnya*.

55. The three (form, sense-organ and contact) cannot be related, as they have no identity. In the absence of contact feeling would not be possible.

56. Consciousness arises in relativity to internal and external bases. Thus consciousness is unreal like mirage and magic.

57. The object of cosciousness being relative to consciousness cannot exist apart from consciousness. A conscious person cannot be there, unless an object and its consciousness are available. Thus conscious person has no identity.

58. Everything is non-eternal in relativity, but in reality nothing could be eternal or non-eternal. An existent thing would be either eternal or non-eternal. But how would this be possible?

59. Since attachment, aversion and delusion originate in relativity to perversion in respect of good, bad things, attachment, aversion and delusion are devoid of identity.

60. One and the same thing can become an object of attachment, aversion and delusion. Therefore, they are mental constructions which are not real.

61. That which is mentally constructed has no existence. But how could there be mental construction unless there be a thing so constructed? As that which is constructed and the construction are relative, they are *s'ūnya.*

62. Ignorance arising from perversion of four kinds, is annihilated by the knowledge of truth. In the absence of ignorance impressions would not arise. So would other links.

63. Things originating in relativity to this or that entity would cease to be when those entities do not exist. Existence, non-existence; composite and non-composite are all being calm extinguished.

64. The Master says that existence dependent upon cause and relativity, when constructed mentally to be real, is ignorance. From this arise twelve links.

65. He who by seeing properly knows that thingsare *s'ūnya* becomes free from delusion. This is the cessation of ignorance. Thereupon all the eleven remaining links would cease.

66. The impressions are like a city appearing in the sky, magic, mirage, floating hair, foam, bubble, artificially created beings, dream and wheels of firebrand.

67. Existence has no identity, nor is there non-existence. Existence and non-existence being dependent upon causes and relativity are *s'ūnya*.

68. The incomparable Buddha taught relative origination of all things. Therefore, all things are devoid of identity.

69. This is what is the ultimate meaning of his teachings. The perfect Lord viewed this multi-faceted world consisting in the transaction people undertake.

70. He did not go against worldly transaction. But he in the ultimate sense did not teach any truth. The fools do not understand what he taught and thus become frightened by the teaching, free from blemish.

71. He did not reject the worldly principle: 'This being there, that arises'. But anything that is relative cannot have identity; it cannot certainly have existence.

72. He who with reverence tries to seek the truth; he who is conscious this way of teaching logically and thus realizes that there is nothing which has any base, overcomes the cycles of birth and death and becomes calm.

73. The nets of bad views vanish by understanding 'This is relative to that'. Thus unsullied one attains Nirvāṇa by overcoming attachment, aversion and delusion.

NĀGĀRJUNA

A TREATISE ON THE REJECTION OF CONTENTIONS

Objections Against the Mādhayamika Position

1. If all the things, everywhere, have no identity (*svabhāva*) your statement being devoid of identity would be incapable of controverting identity.

2. If this statement were to have identity, your former proposition would be contradicted. It would become inconsistent and you have to state the reason for this distinction.

3. If you think that this is like 'Do not make a sound', this is not justified. Here a sound while in existence prevents any sound in the future.

4. If you think that the negation of the statement negating identity would also be like this, then this is not true. This way your proposition is rendered defective on account of its characteristics (*lakṣaṇataḥ*), not mine.

5. If you reject things after apprehending them through perception, then there is no such perception which could comprehend things.

6. With the refutation of perception, inference, verbal testimony and comparison, as well as things established by inference, verbal testimony and examples are refuted.

7. The people who know the state of existence think that good things have good for their identity. This applies to remaining things.

8. Things mentioned in the context of the state of existence, like those leading to emancipation, have emancipatory

identity. So are the things not leading to emancipation, and so on.

9. If things have no identity they are identitiless. But they would not even bear the name 'identitiless' as no name without there being a thing is possible.

10. If the existence of identity is accepted but the same is held to be not belonging to things, then identity would be not belonging to a thing. It would be proper if that to which identity belongs is mentioned.

11. Negation is found applying only to existing things, as in 'There is no pot in the house'. This being so, to you this negation would be of an existent identity.

12. If there is no identity, what do you negate by this statement. The negation of a non-existent thing is established without a statement.

13. Just as ignorant people wrongly see water in mirage, similarly when you negate non-existent things, you see wrongly.

14. This being so there would exist six things: viz. seeing, an object seen and the one who sees; likewise, negation, what is negated and the one who negates.

15. If these seeing, the object seen and the one who sees do not exist. then in the same way negation, what is negated and the one who negates would not exist.

16. If negation, what is negated and the one who negates do not exist, then all things and their very identity are established.

17. In your case no reason can be established; how could there be a reason for you, as it would be without identity. It is not justified to hold a thing without idenitity as established.

18. If for you the rejection of identity could be established without reason, then for me also the existence of identity would be established without reason.

19. To hold that the existence of reason consists in identitilessness of things, is not justified, because there is nothing in all the worlds devoid of identity.

20. It is also not justified to hold that negation comes first and the thing negated afterwards, or it comes after the things negated, or simultaneously with it; because identity continues existing.

Rejection of Contentions

21. If my statement does not exist in the totality of causes and relativity, it being *s'ūnya* is established because things have no identity.

22. Being in relativity is what is called *s'ūnyatā*; what exists being relative is no-identity.

23. Just as a person artificially created were to negate another person whom he, in his turn, has created by his magic, similar would be this negation.

24. This statement has no identity, therefore, there is no abandoning my position. It is also not inconsistent and no special reason need be stated.

25. The example of 'Do not make a sound' which is brought out by you is not appropriate, because there sound is employed to prevent sound. But here the case is not of that kind.

26. If it could be possible to prevent an identitiless thing by another identitiless means, then on account of the rejection of identitilessness identity would stand established.

27. Or it would be like a person holding, in respect of an artificially created woman, 'This is a woman', and his wrong notion being dispelled by another artificially created person.

28. Or this reason would be similar to what is yet to be established, as sound has no existence and we speak not irrespective of usage.

29. If there be any proposition made by me, this accusation would apply. But since I have no proposition, I do not stand accused.

30. If I were to find something by means of perception etc. I would affirm or deny it. But as it is not so, the accusation does not apply to me.

31. If individual things were to be established by means of evidences (*pramāṇa*), then, say, how are those evidences to be established for you.

32. If other evidences were to establish those evidences, it would become an endless series. There neither the first is established, nor the middle, nor the last.

33. If they were established without evidences, then the position is abandoned. There would be inconsistency in it; for their distinction reason has to be stated.

34. This one is an inconsistent argument: Fire does not illumine itself, because its absence is not seen as is the absence of a pot seen in darkness.

35. If, as you say, this fire were to illumine itself, then fire would burn itself as it burns others.

36. If, as you say, fire illumines itself and others, then darkness, like fire, would engulf both itself and others.

37. Darkness does not exist in fire, nor it exists elsewhere where fire exists. How could fire illumine darkness, as

illumination means destruction of darkness.

38. It is wrong to say that fire illumines as soon as it originates. This is because as soon as fire originates, it does not find darkness.

39. Or if without meeting darkness fire were to destroy darkness, then fire placed here would destroy darkness in all the worlds.

40. If according to you evidences were established by themselves, then, for you, evidences would be established irrespective of objects of evidences. What is established by itself is not dependent on others.

41. If according to you 'evidences are established irrespective of the objects', then this kind of evidences would not belong to anything.

42. If your view is that evidences are established depending upon their objects, what is wrong with it? It will be establishing what is already established, as that which is not established cannot depend upon others.

43. If ultimately evidences are established depending upon their object, then the establishment of objects would be without their dependence on evidences.

44. If objects are established not by dependence upon evidences, then what have you to do with the establishment of evidences? The purpose, in that case, for which evidences are required is already achieved.

45. If according to you the establishment of evidences is done only by their dependence on their objects, then evidences and objects would certainly interchange.

46. If in your view objects were to be established by the establishment of evidences and evidences were to be established by the establishment of object, then, for you both of them would remain unestablished.

47. If evidences were to establish object but these evidences themselves were to be established by those very objects, then how would those objects establish them?

48. If objects were to establish evidences, but those objects were to be established by those very evidences, then how would those evidences establish them?

49. If a father were to cause the birth of a son and that very son were to cause the birth of that father, then, say, who would give birth to whom?

50. Now tell, who would be the father and who the son, because both of them have the characteristics of father and son. We have doubt on this point.

51. Evidences are not established by themselves, nor are they established by each other; they are not established by some other evidences, not also by objects and not even accidentally.

52. If the people who know the state of existence say that good things have good as identity, this ought to have been stated distinctly.

53. If good as identity were to arise in relativity, it would become 'other'to good things. How could identity be like that?

54. If good as identity of good things were to arise not in relativity to anything, then no staying with the preceptor would be effective.

55. There would be no merit or demerit; no worldy transactions (vyavahāra). Things with identity would be eternal, as those which have no cause are eternal.

56. Similar defect would arise in respect of bad and indeterminate things and things leading to emancipation etc. For you, thus, all composite (*saṃskṛta*) entities would very much become non-composite (*a-saṃskṛta*).

57. He who says that a name is existent, to him you can react by saying that it would have identity. But we do not say a name to be so.

58. Is this name 'non-existent' whether the name of an existing thing or of a non-existing thing? In both the cases, i.e. be it a name of an existent or of a non-existent entity, your position is untenable.

59. We have already explained that all the entities are *śūnya* This, therefore, is an accusation for the position not taken.

60. The objection raised by saying: 'If existence of identity is accepted, but the same is held to be not belonging to things' is no objection.

61. If only the existent can be negated, then this *śūnyatā* is established, because you are negating identitilessness of existing things.

62. You are negating *s'ūnyatā*, but that *s'ūnyatā* does not exist. This being the case your view that negation pertains to existents becomes contradicted.

63. I do not negate anything; there is nothing to be negated. Therefore, you are falsely accusing me for negating.

64. You said: without any statement the negation of a non-esistent thing is established. Here the statement states that a thing does not exist. This statement does not remove a thing. Thus what you say is not so.

65. Again, pertaining to that great debate you have introduced of the example of mirage, listen to the decision as to how that example is justified.

66. If seeing were to be in identity, it would not originate in relativity. The thing originating in relativity is *śunyata* itself.

67. If seeing were to have identity, who could remove that seeing? This holds good in respect of remaining things.

Therefore, this is no accusation.

68. Thus also is rejected the absence of reason. It is similar to the line stated earlier in the context of the rejection of the example of mirage etc.

69. The reason concerning three times advanced by you has been refuted for being; similar to what is yet to be established. The reason denying three times holds good for those who proclaim *s'ūnyatā*.

70. To whom this *s'ūnyatā* is effective, to him all the matters become effective. To whom this *s'ūnyatā* is not effective nothing becomes effective.

71. He who proclaimed *s'ūnyatā*, relative origination and the Middle Path to be the same, I bow down to that incomparable Buddha, the Enlightened.

NĀGĀRJUNA

VIGRAHA-VYĀVARTANĪ-KĀRIKĀḤ

1. sarveṣāṃ bhāvānām sarvatra na vidyate svabhāvaś cet/
tvadvacanam asvabhāvaṃ na nivartayituṃ svabhāvam alam//

2. atha sasvabhāvam etad vākyaṃ pūravā hatā pratijñā te/
vaiṣamikatvaṃ tasmin viśeṣahetuś ca vaktavyaḥ//

3. mā śabdavad ity etat syāt te buddhir na caitad upapannam/
śabdena hy atra satā bhaviṣyato vāraṇaṃ tasya//

4. pratiṣedhapratiṣedho 'py evam iti matam bhavet tad asad eva/
evam tava pratijñā lakṣaṇato dūṣyate na mama//

5. pratyakṣeṇa hi tāvad yady upalabhya vinivartayasi bhāvān/
tan nāsti pratyakṣam bhāvā yenopalabhyante//

6. anumānaṃ pratyuktaṃ pratyakṣeṇāgamopamāne ca/
anumānāgamasādhyā ye 'rthā dṛṣṭāntasādhyāś ca//

7. kuś'alānāṃ dharmāvasthāvidaś ca manyante/
kuśalaṃ janāḥ svabhāvaṃ śeṣeṣv apy eṣa viniyogaḥ//

8. nairyāṇikasvabhāvo dharmā nairyāṇikās' ca ye teṣām/
dharmāvasthoktānām evam anairyānikādīnām//

9. yadi ca na bhavet svabhāvo dharmāṇāṃ niḥsvabhāva ity evam/
nāmāpi bhaven naivaṃ nāma hi nirvastukaṃ nāsti//

10. atha vidyate svabhāvaḥ sa ca dharmānāṃ na vidyate tasmāt/
dharmair vinā svabhāvaḥ sa yasya tad yuktam upadeṣṭum//

11. sata eva pratiṣedho nāsti ghaṭo geha ity ayaṃ yasmāt/
drṣṭaḥ pratiṣedho 'yam sataḥ svabhāvasya te tasmāt//

12. atha nāsti sa svabhāvaḥ kiṃ nu pratiṣidhyate tvayānena/
vacanenarte vacanāt pratiṣedhaḥ sidhyate hy asataḥ//

13. bālānām iva mithyā mṛgatṛṣṇāyāṃ yathā jalagrāhaḥ/
evaṃ mithyāgrāhaḥ syāt te pratiṣedhayato hy asataḥ//

14. nanv evaṃ saty asti grāho grāhyaṃ ca tadgrahītā ca/
pratiṣedhaḥ pratiṣedhyaṃ pratiṣeddhā ceti ṣaṭkaṃ tat//

15. atha naivāsti grāho naiva grāhyaṃ na ca grahītāraḥ/
pratiṣedhaḥ pratiṣedhyaṃ pratiṣeddhāro nanu na santi//

16. pratiṣedhaḥ pratiṣedhyaṃ pratiṣeddhāras' ca yady uta na santi/
siddhā hi sarvabhāvās teṣām eva svabhāvas' ca//

17. hetos' ca te na siddhir naiḥsvābhāvyāt kuto hi te hetuḥ/
nirhetukasya siddhir na copapannāsya te 'rthasya//

18. yadi cāhetoḥ siddhiḥ svabhāvavinivartanasya te bhavati/
svābhāvyasyāstivaṃ mamāpi nirhetukaṃ sidham//

19. atha hetor astitvaṃ bhāvasvābhāvyam ity anupapannam/
lokeṣu niḥsvabhāvo na hi kas' cana vidyate bhāvaḥ//

20. pūrvam cet pratiṣedhaḥ pas'cāt pratiṣedhyam ity anupapannam/
paścāc cānupapanno yugapac ca yataḥ svabhāvaḥ san//

21. hetupratyayasāmagryāṃ ca pṛthak cāpi madvaco na yadi/
nanu śūnyatvaṃ sidhaṃ bhāvānām asvabhāvatvāt//

22. yaś ca pratītya bhāvo bhāvānāṃ s'ūnyateti sā prokatā/
yaś ca pratītyabhāvo bhavati hi tasyāsvabhāvatvaṃ//

23. nirmitako nirmitakaṃ māyāpuruṣaḥ svamāyayā sṛṣṭam/
pratiṣedhayeta yadvat pratiṣedho 'yaṃ tathaiva syāt//

24. na svābhāvikam etad vākyaṃ tasmān na vādahānir me/
nāsti ca vaiṣamikatvaṃ viśeṣahetuś ca na nigādyaḥ//

25. mā śabdavad iti nāyaṃ dṛṣṭanto yas tvayā samārabdhaḥ/
śabdena hi tac chabdasya vāraṇaṃ naivam etac ca//

26. naiḥsvābhāvyānāṃ cen naiḥsvābhāvyena vāraṇaṃ yadi hi/
naiḥsvābhāvyanivṛttau svābhāvyaṃ hi prasiddhaṃ syāt//

27. atha vā nirmitakāyāṃ yathā striyāṃ strīyam ity asadgrāham/
nirmitakaḥ pratihanyāt kasya cid evaṃ bhaved etat//

28. atha vā sādhyasamo 'yaṃ hetur na hi vidyate dhvaneḥ sattā/
saṃvyavahāraṃ ca vayaṃ nānabhyupagamya kathayāmaḥ//

29. yadi kā cana pratijñā syān me tata eṣa me bhaved doṣaḥ/
nāsti ca mama pṛtijñā tasmān naivāsti me doṣaḥ//

30. yadi kiṃ cid upalabheyaṃ pravartayeyaṃ nivartayeyaṃ vā/
pratyakṣādibhir arthais tadabhāvan me 'nupālambhaḥ//

31. yadi ca pramāṇatas te teṣāṃ teṣāṃ prasiddhir arthānām/
teṣāṃ punaḥ prasiddhiṃ brūhi kathaṃ te pramāṇānām//

32. anyair yadi pramāṇaiḥ pramāṇasiddhir bhavet tad anavasthā/
nādeḥ siddhis tatrāsti naiva madhyasya nāntasya//

33. teṣām atha pramāṇair vinā prasiddhir vihīyate vādaḥ/
vaiṣamikātvaṃ tasmin viśeṣahetuś ca vaktavyaḥ//

34. viṣamopanyāso'yaṃ na hy ātmānam prakāś'ayaty agniḥ/
na hi tasyānupalabdhir dṛṣṭā tamasīva kumbhasya//

35. yadi ca svātmānam ayaṃ tvadvacanena prakāś'ayati agniḥ/
param iva nanav ātmānaṃ svaṃ paridhakṣyaty api hutāśaḥ//

36. yadi ca svaparātmānau tvadvacanena prakāś'ayaty agniḥ/
pracchādayiṣyati tamaḥ svaparātmānau hutāśa iva//

37. nāsti tamaś ca jvalane yatra ca tiṣṭhati parātmani jvalanaḥ/
kurute kathaṃ prakāśam sa hi prakāś'o 'ndhakāravadhaḥ//

38. utpadyamāna eva prakāśayaty agnir ity asadvādaḥ/
utpadyamāna eva prāpnoti tamo na hi hutāś'aḥ//

39. aprāpto 'pi jvalano yadi vā punar andhakāram upahanyāt/
sarveṣu lokadhātuṣu tamo 'yam iha saṃsthito hanyāt//

40. yadi svataś' ca pramāṇasiddhir anapekṣya tava prameyāṇi/
bhavati pramāṇasiddhir na parāpekṣā svataḥsiddhiḥ//

41. anapekṣya hi prameyān arthān yadi te pramāṇasiddhir iti/
na bhavanti kasya cid evam imāni tāni pramāṇāni//

42. atha matam apekṣya siddhis teṣām ity atra bhavati ko doṣaḥ/
siddhasya sādhanaṃ syān nāsiddho 'pekṣate hy anyat//

43. sidhyanti hi prameyāṇy apekṣya yadi sarvathā pramāṇāni/
bhavati prameyasiddhir nāpekṣyaiva pramāṇāni//

44. yadi ca prameyasiddhir nāpekṣyaiva bhavati pramāṇāni/
kiṃ te pramāṇasiddhyā tāni yadartham prasiddhaṃ tat//

45. atha tu pramāṇasiddhir bhavaty apekṣyaiva te prameyāṇi/
vyatyaya evaṃ sati te dhruvaṃ pramāṇaprameyāṇām//

46. atha te pramāṇasiddhyā prameyasiddhiḥ prameyasiddhyā ca/
bhavati pramāṇasiddhir nāsty ubhayasyāpi te siddhiḥ//

47. sidhyanti hi pramāṇair yadi prameyāṇi tāni tair eva /
sādhyāni ca prameyais tāni kathaṃ sādhayiṣyanti//

48. sidhyanti ca prameyair yadi pramāṇāni tāni tair eva/
sādhyāni ca pramāṇais tāni kathaṃ sādhāyiṣyanti//

49. pitrā yady utpādyaḥ putro yadi tena caiva putreṇa/
utpādyah sa yadi pitā vada tatrotpādayati kaḥ kam//

50. kas' ca pitā kaḥ putras tatra tvaṃ brūhi tāv ubhāv api ca/
pitṛputralakṣaṇadharau yato bhavati no 'tra saṃdehaḥ//

51. naiva svataḥ prasiddhir na parasparataḥ parapramāṇair vā/
na bhavati na ca prameyair na cāpy akasmāt pramāṇānām//

52. kuśalānāṃ dharmāṇāṃ dharmāvasthāvido bruvīran yat/
kuśalaṃ svabhāvam evaṃ pravibhāgenābhidheyaḥ syāt//

53. yadi ca pratītya kus'alaḥ svabhāva utpadyate sa kus'alānām/
dharmāṇāṃ parabhāvaḥ svabhāva evaṃ kathaṃ bhavati//

54. atha na pratītya kiṃ cit svabhāva utpadyate sa kuśalānām/
dharmāṇāṃ evaṃ syād vāso na brahmacaryasya//

55. nādharmo dharmo vā saṃvyavahāraś ca laukikā na syuḥ/
nityās' ca sasvabhāvāḥ syur nityatvād ahetumataḥ//

56. evam akus'aleṣv avyākṛteṣu nairyāṇikādiṣu ca doṣaḥ/
tasmāt sarvaṃ saṃskṛtam asaṃskṛtaṃ te bhavaty eva//

57. yaḥ sadbhūtaṃ nāmātra brūyat sasvabhāva ity evam/
bhavatā prativaktavyo nāma brūmas' ca na vayaṃ sat//

58. nāmāsad iti ca yad idaṃ tat kiṃ nu sato bhavaty utāpy asataḥ/
yadi hi sato yady asato dvidhāpi te hīyate vādaḥ//

59. sarveṣām bhāvānām s'ūnyatvaṃ copapāditaṃ pūrvam/
sa upālambhas tasmād bhavaty ayaṃ cāpratijñāyāḥ//

60. atha vidyate svabhāvaḥ sa ca dharmāṇāṃ na vidyata itīdam/
ās'aṅkitam yad uktaṃ bhavaty anās'aṅkitaṃ tac ca//

61. sata eva pratiṣedho yadi s'ūnyatvam nanu prasiddham idam/
pratiṣedhayate hi bhavān bhavānāṃ niḥsvabhavatvam///

62. pratiṣedhayase 'tha tvaṃ śūnyatvam tac ca nāsti s'ūnyatvam/
pratiṣedhaḥ sata iti te nanv eṣa vihīyate vādaḥ//

63. pratiṣedhayāmi nāhaṃ kiṃ cit pratiṣedhyam asti na ca kiṃ cit/
tasmāt pratiṣedhayasīty adhilaya eṣa tvayā kriyate//

64. yac cāharte vacanād asataḥ pratiṣedhavacanasiddhir iti/
atra jñāpayate vāg asad iti tan na pratinihanti//

65. mṛgatṛṣṇādṛṣṭānte yaḥ punar uktas tvayā mahāṃaś carcaḥ/
tatrāpi nirṇayaṃ śṛṇu yathā sa dṛṣṭānta upapannaḥ//

66. sa yadi svabhāvataḥ syād grāho na syāt pratītya saṃbhūtaḥ/
yaś ca pratītya bhavati grāho nanu śūnyatā saiva//

67. yadi ca svabhāvataḥ syād grāhaḥ kas taṃ nivartayed grāham/
śeṣeṣv apy eṣa vidhis tasmād eṣo 'nupalambhaḥ//

68. etena hetvabhāvaḥ pratyuktaḥ purvam eva sa samatvāt/
mṛgatṛṣṇādṛṣṭāntavyāvṛttividhau ya uktaḥ prāk//

69. yas traikalye hetuḥ pratyuktaḥ pūrvam eva sa samatvāt/
traikālyapratihetuś ca śūnyatāvādinaṃ prāptaḥ//

70. prabhavati ca śūnyateyam yasya prabhavanti tasya sarvārthāḥ/
prabhavati na tasya kiṃ cin na prabhavati śūnyatā yasya//

71. yaḥ śūnyatāṃ pratītyasamutpādaṃ madhyamāṃ pratipadaṃ ca/
ekārthaṃ nijagāda praṇamāmi tam apratimabuddham//

INDEX OF KĀRIKĀS